Beyond the
Turning Point

Beyond the Turning Point

The U.S. Economy in the 1980s

Ezra Solomon

W. H. Freeman and Company
San Francisco

This book was published originally as a part
of *The Portable Stanford*, a series of books
published by the Stanford Alumni
Association, Stanford, California.

Library of Congress Cataloging in Publication Data

Solomon, Ezra
    Beyond the turning point.

    Bibliography: p.
    Includes index.
    1.   United States—Economic condition—1971–
2.   United States—Economic policy—1971–   . I.
Title.
HC106.S6   338.973   81–19542
ISBN 0–7167–1390–x   AACR2
ISBN 0–7167–1391–8 (pbk.)

Printed in the United States of America

1 2 3 4 5 6 7 8 9 0   MP   0 8 9 8 7 6 5 4 3 2

To Janet
with my love and affection

CONTENTS

PREFACE

By any measure, the flow of news out of Washington, D.C., in 1981 signaled a historic turning point in the thrust of U.S. economic policy. In a rapid succession of moves, the new Reagan administration reversed the basic direction along which all major manifestations of policy had been moving, in some cases for several decades. The rate of taxation on income was cut sharply, especially on income derived from capital; the share of defense expenditures in the budget was increased and the growth of nondefense spending substantially reduced; the steady trend toward a growing regulatory intervention in the private economy was reversed; finally, the conduct of the nation's monetary policy was directed, quite unequivocally, toward the goal of price stability as opposed to other objectives such as the stabilization of interest rates and exchange rates.

Will the turn in policy bring about the desired turn in economic performance? Given the long lags between policy and performance, we will not know the answer to this question for several years. In 1984 the nation will cast its vote on whether the results of the policies begun in 1981 are promising enough to warrant continuation. In the interim there will be daily, weekly, and monthly evaluations of how well or poorly this decisive reversal of policies is serving the economy.

What follows is an intelligent layman's guide to how and why we got to where we are on the economic front; to what the change in economic policy of 1981 is all about; and to where it might lead in the future.

Ezra Solomon

Stanford, California
September 28, 1981

'Bomb threat'

Drawing by Eric Smith
Courtesy Capital-Gazette (Md.) Newspapers

1

Two Views of the 1980s

FOR THE U.S. ECONOMY, the long trend of good performance during what we called the postwar period ended in the early 1970s when three major sets of problems that had been brewing for years matured, converged, and blew up in our faces: the problem of inflation, the energy problem and its consequences, and finally the problem of a government increasingly incapable of controlling its budget or of dealing with any large problem incisively because its own swollen political agenda kept getting in the way.

Powerful interactions among this ugly triplet of problems caused the many traumas we suffered between 1973 and 1980—a huge increase in the level of prices and interest rates, two massive jumps in the price of oil, severe recessions and feeble recoveries, a large drop in the dollar's exchange rate, and painful losses for all who held financial assets denominated in U.S. dollars.

As we move into the 1980s, there are two economic scenarios being forecast for the decade ahead. One is that it will be a replay of what occurred in the 1970s. If this projection is correct, the outlook for the decade is an extremely gloomy one indeed.

The second and more optimistic view is that far from being the most likely scenario for the 1980s, a replay of the 1970s is in fact the least likely one. This view is based on the idea that policies determine future trends and that we have reached a major turning point in economic policy. By the end of 1980, most Americans realized that a continuation along the economic road we had followed in the 1970s would lead to grave dangers in the future. The advent of new leadership in the White House and the Senate offered a turning point from that road and a good chance for a successful return to orderly, noninflationary growth. Would intellectual and political inertia permit us to take that turn and to pursue the new policies that were put forward in early 1981? More importantly, would the turn in policy bring with it the desired return of good economic performance?

I do not pretend to see the future clearly and right now nobody does. But we have to travel into the future. We also have to make decisions on the basis of facts we have not yet seen. As a villager in the Himalayas once told me, "I have not climbed this mountain before; in fact I don't know exactly where I am because I have not been here before either. But I do know mountains, and I will keep you company, and who knows—I may show you a wild flower or two."

Performance Deteriorates

The first 25 years after World War II was an excellent period for the U.S. economy. By any overall measure of economic and financial performance it was one of the best quarter centuries in our history. The same was true for most of the other industrial economies of the world. In sharp contrast, the 1970s gave us our worst economic performance for any decade since the 1930s. A previously well-functioning system whose growth and stability we had taken for granted began to unravel just before the 1970s began, and things became steadily worse over the next ten years.

When we finally closed the books on the decade in the last quarter of 1980, it was already clear to most of the country that the U.S. economy had fared very poorly on all of three dimensions that jointly comprise our economic well-being—the real dimension, the financial dimension, and the dimension of public confidence.

Real Results

Economists use the word *real* to describe what remains after the effects of inflation have been removed. Within this world of real measures a key number is the rate of productivity—the level of useful output produced per hour of work. On it depends that elusive thing we call our standard of living.

For 20 years prior to 1968, productivity in the private business sector of the U.S. grew by just over 3 percent a year. Though it seems like a small number, at that rate, assuming the fraction of the total population working remains about the same, average living standards double every 22 years. In just one century, material standards per capita will rise by a factor of 20. At that rate of development everybody in Papua, New Guinea, in the year 2080 would be 50 percent better off than the average Australian is today.

There is another, broader measure of productivity, namely, output—or real gross national product (GNP)—per person employed. This measure allows for the fact that as societies become richer they permit themselves shorter hours of work per week, more vacations per year, and more social, environmental, and governmental services. By this alternative measure of productivity the U.S. achieved a steady compound improvement of around 2.5 percent a year for the 20 years prior to 1968, a rate large enough to allow a doubling of measured per capita living standards with each new generation (estimated to be around 27 years for the U.S.) even while enjoying large increases in leisure and governmental services.

The record for the 1970s was vastly different. In fact it was terrible. For the decade as a whole, the increase in output per person employed was so trivial that at such a rate it would take many centuries to achieve the next doubling in our per capita living standards. The record during the final four years of the decade, from December 1976 to December 1980, which happened to coincide with a presidential term, was abysmal—the level of output per hour of work was no higher at the end of the four-year period than it had been at the beginning. If we were to continue on this path of stagnant productivity for the next 35 years, and if the inhabitants of Singapore do in the future as well as we did from 1948 to 1968 (a standard they have been surpassing), the average child born in Singapore in 1980 would by age 35 have a higher economic standard of living than his or her U.S. contemporary!

Financial Results

As is the case in any urban society, households in the U.S. hold a large part of their wealth in the form of financial assets—that is, paper assets denominated in U.S. dollars. We held some $4 *trillion* in this form as of December 1980. During the 1970s the average dollar so held delivered a sizeable *loss* to its owner instead of the decent gain it had delivered during the 1950s and 1960s. Some who had saved and had held their savings in financial assets such as bank accounts, savings accounts, U.S. savings bonds, or corporate bonds suffered severe losses. Others who were more worldly-wise and chose to put their funds into common stocks did almost as badly.

Psychological Results

Confidence in the future is an important dimension of our economic well-being. The events of the 1970s seriously eroded both the confidence and the sense of well-being we enjoyed in the late 1960s. By the end of 1980 an economy we had thought of as reasonably predictable just a dozen years earlier had become an economy characterized by disorder and uncertainty, with large segments of it in a state of serious disarray. The slide of a normally optimistic people and a hitherto ascendant economy into a defensive pessimism showed up as clearly on Wall Street as it did in Washington, D.C., or Detroit.

The nation's largest stockbroker used to call attention to its services by displaying a thundering herd of bulls. By 1980 the advertisement showed only a single bull; frequently he was in a cave and sometimes it was raining outside. The message was shelter. In Detroit, an industry that was once the vanguard in the battle for open competition and free trade was also seeking shelter. The auto industry argument against imports was not the traditional litany—foreign government subsidies, or dumping, or unfair competition from "cheap" labor; it was simply that the Japanese had become too efficient at making small, fuel-efficient cars. In Washington the industry of modern political government was seeking shelter from problems that it had itself created. Its own budget was out of control as were the actions of regulators who enforced the spate of hastily written laws that 15 years of political activism had spawned. A divided electorate, whose polarization into special-interest groups politicians themselves had encouraged in order to get and keep votes, had become far less predictable at the polls. The constant need for a modern politician to keep one ear to the ground in order to stay in office ran hard against the realization that it was extremely difficult to lead from that position.

Interpreting the Seventies

What switched the U.S. economy from a track of excellent performance to the opposite track of very poor performance? What does the recent record imply for the 1980s?

As always there are at least as many forecasts of the future as there are forecasters. In these days of computer printouts there are sometimes twice as many forecasts as there are forecasters. And, as always, how the forecasters see the future depends on how they interpret the past. For present purposes we can divide all of them into two broad groups:

1. The first group interprets what happened in the 1970s as the beginning of a new and adverse long-term trend. The forecast implied by

this view is that the 1980s will bring a replay of the 1970s. I label this the *replay* view.

2. A second group interprets what happened in the 1970s not as a new trend but rather as a prolonged series of adjustments and responses to huge imbalances that government policy itself had created in the 1960s and stubbornly continued to magnify in the 1970s. In this view, a replay of the 1970s is the least likely scenario for the 1980s—indeed we are more likely to see a decisive turnaround in policy and an about-face in economic and financial behavior. I label this the *turnaround* view.

The Replay View

The essence of the replay forecast is simple: The favorable trend in the U.S. economy during the postwar period ended in the early 1970s; what has been happening since then marks the start of a new and adverse long-term trend that will persist through the 1980s. If this diagnosis and projection are correct, the outlook for the decade ahead is bleak: high and probably accelerating rates of inflation; high and probably even higher rates of interest; a continued decline in productivity gains at home and a generally falling but highly unstable dollar abroad; more large jumps in the price of OPEC oil; more losses for those who hold their wealth in paper assets denominated in U.S. dollars; and, finally, a continuation of significant federal government budget deficits year after year after year. Indeed, according to an extreme wing of this school of thought there is a high probability that we will witness a serious collapse of our monetary and financial system before the decade is over.

The appeal of the replay scenario is that it is both simple and plausible. It is simple in that it requires little explanation and almost no ifs, ands, or buts in order to jump from diagnosis to prognostication. A trend is a trend and all we have to do to see into the future is to project a continuation of the recent past. The replay scenario is also plausible in that it smacks of hardheaded realism—it assumes simply that one has only to look at what actually happened during the 1970s to know what the future will bring.

The trouble with the replay scenario is suggested by H.L. Mencken's quip: "For every difficult problem there is always an easy answer—simple, plausible, and *wrong*." Being simplistic and hardheaded is not in itself a basis for prescience; nor is a simple projection of recent experience a sure road into the future. As Disraeli said in one of those delightfully self-contradictory statements that confound and amuse philosophers, "We learn from history that we do not learn from history." In other words, projecting the future from the recent past is sometimes sensible; at other times it is absurd. The trick lies in knowing the difference between a trend and an aberration.

The Turnaround View

The alternative view of what happened to the U.S. economy in the 1970s, and hence the alternative view of what the 1980s might bring, is that the 1970s did *not* mark the beginning of a new trend, and hence the economic performance between 1969 and 1980 cannot be projected to continue into the future.

In this view, a quarter-century trend of favorable economic and financial performance did end in the early 1970s, but it ended for reasons of our own making. Three major imbalances, all of them created largely by our own policies, for years had been allowed to become progressively worse. In the early 1970s they matured one by one, and the economy crumbled under their combined weight. The three problems were (1) inflation—a problem that only governments can create; (2) rising U.S. dependence on energy imports and the consequent rapid transformation around 1970 of a buyer's market for oil into a seller's market—a transformation in which our own policies played a large role; and (3) a government that was unable to recognize or deal incisively either with inflation or our growing energy dependence because of its own swollen political agenda. What we witnessed in the 1970s was a series of violent but nonetheless transitory adjustments to these imbalances.

There are two explanations for why the pain of adjustment has continued for so long. One explanation is that the two basic imbalances reinforced one another: In 1973 and again in 1979 U.S. inflation and the large devaluations of the dollar that followed were part of the cause for large jumps in oil prices; these jumps, in turn, exacerbated the worldwide rate of inflation. A second and more fundamental explanation is that governmental policies here and abroad tried to shield key segments of society from the economic pain that the adjustment process might inflict on them. In the process, policy simply prolonged old imbalances and created new ones that required further corrections. For example, we suppressed domestic oil and gas prices in order to blunt the impact of OPEC's pricing actions on consumers—and thus worsened the degree of our energy dependence, which in turn eventually led to still higher OPEC prices. We tried to blunt the impact of inflation by legislating rapid increases in benefits and wages for those who were least able to protect themselves from inflation—and thus enlarged the size of the federal budget, which in turn led to even more inflation. Just how much longer it will take to complete the already protracted transition depends entirely on the vitality with which U.S. governmental policies are shifted decisively toward hastening, as opposed to hindering, the adjustment process itself. In one sense this is what the Reagan program is all about.

The turnaround view does not have the simplicity of the replay thesis. Indeed it is devilishly complex to understand and even harder to explain. One reason for the complexity is that the world of the 1970s was adjusting not to just one or two but three separate imbalances, each of which was large enough to damage economic performance—the monetary imbalance, which causes rapid price increases; the energy imbalance, which causes wrenching adaptations in industrial societies; and the major imbalances within government policy itself, which retard adjustment and dampen productivity. Furthermore, all three imbalances generate responses that interact powerfully with one another. To understand one set of problems it is necessary to understand them all. And for the government to deal with any one of these problems effectively, it must provide a comprehensive policy addressed to all three.

The Seventies as Trend

The number of "economist" jokes in circulation always rises when the performance of the economy worsens. It is a sign of our times that 1980 was a record year for such jokes. Not only were they more numerous than ever before but they were cruel to boot! In the 1950s, it was alleged that President Eisenhower, frustrated by the habit his economic advisers had of always conditioning their advice by saying, "on the one hand *this*, on the other hand *that*," pleaded for a "one-armed economist." The 1980 version of the tale went as follows: "How do you get a one-armed economist out of a tree?" Answer: "You wave at him!"

When they first appeared in the 1960s, large-scale computer-based econometric models were generally held in great awe by the layman. The economic forecasts they generated sold for tens of thousands of dollars. But as these forecasts went increasingly astray, they too suffered the slings of wit. A recent cartoon shows two bearded economists next to a computer. One says to the other, "This forecasting business is getting difficult." The other replies, "Yeah! Especially if it involves the *future*."

The joke is not as whimsical as it might at first appear. Economists make two quite different kinds of forecasts. The first is the conditional forecast: the "if you do this, that will happen" sort of statement. For example, if you inflate the money supply, you will get price inflation. If you artificially suppress the price of a product, you will increase demand, discourage supply, and eventually suffer shortages of it. If you beat the saver over the head and subsidize the borrower, you will get lots of borrowing and very little saving. The profession has been quite

*"He's considered to be a bellwether in the
field of economic forecasting."*

good at this kind of forecasting; indeed, we have been painfully prophetic. The trouble is that until lately nobody really has listened, especially not politicians.

The second type of forecasting is akin to outright prophecy. The record on this type of forecasting has been mixed. It was good in the 1950s and 1960s but became progressively worse in the 1970s. Mr. G. William Miller, who served as chairman of the Federal Reserve System (1977–79) and as secretary of the Treasury (1979–80)—the two most powerful positions as far as economic policy is concerned—must hold the all-time record for the number of forecasts, revisions to forecasts, and continuously wrong forecasts for any senior economic official in U.S. history. Nonetheless, all of them were listened to, and indeed acted on, by otherwise sensible people.

It is not difficult to see why forecasts in the 1970s went increasingly astray. Although the recipes used for generating forecasts range all the way from simple back-of-the-envelope calculations to vast econometric exercises that solve hundreds of simultaneous equations on a computer, all of them involve just three ingredients. The first ingredient is a flow of reliable statistics about what is happening in the economy. The second is a good understanding of past trends in economic variables and the patterns of relationships among them. The third and critical ingredient is the assumption that these patterns and trends will persist into the future, i.e., that we live in a world of continuity.

When the statistical record is reliable and the trends and patterns do in fact repeat themselves, most forecasting recipes work like a charm and economists do indeed look like prophets. If the data are wrong or misleading and trends and patterns do not repeat themselves, the recipes break down and we tend to look more like one-armed economists in trees who wave back at strangers.

For example, in 1953 the staff of the Joint Economic Committee of the Congress produced and published the first long-range forecast for the U.S. economy. It was a projection of the real* gross national product of the United States for the year 1965, twelve years into the future. The forecast used the simplest of models with none of the elaborations we engage in today. Yet it hit its target square in the bull's-eye. It was even more accurate than the forecasts for 1965 that were made during the course of that year.

The success of the committee's growth projection of 3.5 percent per annum quite naturally led to the idea that there was a predictable underlying long-term growth trend along which a healthy U.S. economy

---

*Real GNP is GNP measured in dollars of constant purchasing power.

ought to move. That trend, referred to as the path of potential growth, became a major guide to national budget and economic policies in the 1960s. It was revised from time to time on the basis of a growing stock of information on the sources of economic growth.

In 1969, after careful study, the officially projected long-term growth rate for the U.S. economy was revised upward to 4.3 percent a year. According to that projection the real GNP of the U.S. in 1979 (assuming it was a year of full employment) should have risen by 59 percent over the level achieved in 1968, the benchmark year on which the projection was based. The actual GNP for 1979 (which *was* a year of full employment) was only 37 percent higher than it had been in 1968. The real long-term growth rate turned out to be not 4.3 percent but 2.8 percent. The projected rate was too high by about 60 percent—a huge error for a real number.

What went wrong? The answer is simple: The projection made in 1953 assumed continuity and the assumption held; the projection made in 1969 also assumed continuity but this time the assumption did not hold. Somewhere in the early 1970s the economy ran into a zone of discontinuity. The big problem was not the employment factor, which rose even faster than had been assumed. It was productivity, which rose far more slowly in the 1970s than anybody guessed in 1968.

What applied to trends applied as strongly to short-run patterns. As the economy itself moved into a state of disarray in the 1970s, the very foundation on which good forecasting rests crumbled. In a world of rapid inflation, spiraling energy prices, and floating exchange rates, the orderly patterns observed in the 1950s and 1960s no longer repeated themselves. The statistics, bloated by rapid inflation rates, no longer measured the real economic variables with reasonable accuracy. Early in the 1970s we crossed a major historical watershed into a zone in which many of the postwar relationships were no longer valid—a region of discontinuity and disarray.

Financial Forecasts

The path of economic growth is of enormous importance to those who make policy, but the public is generally more interested in projections of other variables such as the rate of inflation, interest rates, the price of common stocks or gold or foreign currencies, and, in recent years, the price of oil. The conventional basis for forecasting these variables—namely, the assumption that the future will generally repeat the past—turned out to be dramatically wrong in the 1970s. To see just how wrong it is possible to be about the future, let us place ourselves back in 1968 and play the game of looking forward to 1980, twelve years into the future. I call this a game, but it is a serious game whose outcome can make or break individuals, companies, and even governments. It is also a game most of us must now play in the 1980s with respect to how things might be 10 to 12 years into the future—for play we must in order to decide how we should invest our wealth and conduct our policies.

To keep things manageable let us pick six key variables on which almost everybody speculates:

1. The level of prices as measured by the U.S. Consumer Price Index (CPI), i.e., the rate of inflation.
2. The price of an ounce of gold.
3. The price of a barrel of oil.
4. The exchange rate between a dollar and a Swiss franc.
5. Interest rates.
6. The level of common stock prices.

How would a conventional analysis made in 1968 on the basis of trends observed in the preceding period have projected the values of these key variables for the period 1968–80 and for the year 1980?

1. *Inflation and the Price Level.* Between 1948 and 1968 the U.S. Consumer Price Index rose at an average annual rate of 1.8 percent. The rate accelerated during the Korean War but came back down rapidly after the war ended; it accelerated again with the Vietnam War (to 4 percent in 1968 itself) but the general expectation was that it would come back down again as the war unwound. Excluding the war years, the average annual rise in prices for the 20 years preceding 1968 was 1.2 percent a year. During the six-year period before the Vietnam War (1959–65) it also averaged 1.2 percent. A "logical" conventional projection for the decade of the 1970s (barring a new war) would have been for an average inflation rate to continue at about the historically observed 1½ percent a year. Hence a projection for the level of the CPI in mid-1980 (based on 1967 = 100 and 1968 = 104) would have been that it would rise by about 20 percent to around 125 on the index.

In fact the CPI in December 1980 was 260! The actual rise in prices for the 12-year period from 1968 to 1980 was 150 percent, as contrasted with a "predicted" rise of 20 percent.

2. *The Price of Gold.* For 55 years between 1879 and 1934 the dollar price of gold was a constant $20.67 per troy ounce. In 1934 the price was moved up irregularly and was then reset at $35 per troy ounce, where it remained until early 1968. During 1968 a free market for gold began and the price moved above the $35 level. It reached $42 for a while but fell back again toward $38 when the International Monetary Fund (IMF)

delayed its decision to buy a million ounces offered to it by South Africa at the official price of $35 an ounce. A prevalent feeling at that time was that speculators had moved free-market prices above $35 largely because guaranteed purchases by the U.S. and the IMF at $35 put a *floor* below which prices could not fall, i.e., speculative losses were limited although gains were not. A lot of people believed that left to a free market the price of gold should rise above $35 to keep pace with general inflation, but even they feared that this could not happen if the largest holders of gold—the central banks of the world—canceled their standing offer to buy unlimited amounts at $35. Thus the conventional forecast for 1980 would have been a split one: The majority, observing the long history of the $35 price prior to 1968, would have guessed $35 for 1980; a minority would have forecast an increase to $50 or even $70 an ounce. The actual peak price of gold in early 1980 was $875 an ounce, and the price around which free-market quotes fluctuated wildly in 1980 was about $600 per ounce.

3. *The Price of Oil.* The situation in the world oil market during the 1950s and 1960s can be characterized as follows: Demand was growing rapidly but supply was growing even faster; prices were weak—the *effective price** of Persian Gulf oil was stuck at around $2.00 a barrel in spite of a gently rising price level for other commodities. Because world oil prices were so depressed, the U.S. protected the domestic oil industry starting in 1959 by imposing a quota restriction on the importation of "cheap" non-U.S. oil. The official purpose was to protect our domestic producing capacity in order to serve our defense capabilities; the real purpose was to subsidize domestic oil refiners who did not have access to low-priced foreign oil.

Foreign producers, notably Iran, tried to get a price higher than $2.00 a barrel for their oil, but none of these attempts succeeded in the 1950s and 1960s. In 1968 a conventional forecaster of the 1980 price of oil at Persian Gulf export points would have guessed $2 to $3 a barrel; someone more in tune with the changing supply/demand relationship might have guessed 50 percent higher, or around $3.50 to $4.50. One or two "madmen" suggested $5 a barrel by 1980. The actual price of Persian Gulf oil in December 1980 was $36 a barrel.

4. *The Dollar/Swiss Franc Exchange Rate.* For at least 30 years prior to 1968, the dollar price of the Swiss franc had been almost constant at around 22.5 U.S. cents per franc. The Swiss franc was the bastion of financial stability in Europe just as the dollar was the bastion of stability

---

*Effective prices are prices actually charged for oil loaded at Persian Gulf ports; they should be distinguished from the posted prices (on which tax revenues are based). See Chapter 4 for a more detailed explanation.

for the free world. These two bastions of value were linked tightly to each other because each was linked to gold. Thus a conventional projection of the exchange value of the Swiss franc for 1980 would have been (and was) 22.5 U.S. cents per Swiss franc, give or take a fraction of a cent. In December 1980 the actual exchange value of a Swiss franc was 60 U.S. cents, nearly three times the projected value.

5. *Interest Rates.* Interest rates are difficult to discuss in summary fashion because there are so many of them. One key rate that is important to investors is the rate offered on long-term (i.e., 25-year maturity) U.S. Treasury bonds. This rate experienced three very lengthy cycles between 1900 and 1968. Starting at around 2.5 percent at the turn of the century, the rate moved up to 5.5 percent in 1920, then down to 2.5 percent in 1941 and up again to 5.5 percent in 1968. The 5.5 percent rate of 1968 was regarded as the *high* end of a historic range. Indeed the law still forbids the Treasury from issuing new long-term bonds that carry a coupon rate in excess of 4.5 percent without a special exemption from the Congress—the idea being that the U.S. should not lock itself into such extraordinary borrowing costs because any rate above 4.5 percent is abnormal and temporary.

In 1968 few people believed that the interest rate on long-term Treasury bonds could get much above 5.5 percent or stay about that level for very long. In fact between 1968 and 1980 it never got *below* 5.5 percent, and in 1980 the Treasury had to offer an interest rate of 12.75 percent in order to market a new issue of 25-year bonds.

6. *Common Stock Prices.* From 1948 to the end of 1968, common stock prices (as measured by the Standard & Poor's 500 stock average) rose almost sevenfold or at an average compound rate of 10 percent a year. During those 20 years the Consumer Price Index rose less than 2 percent a year, so stock prices rose at a *real* rate of over 8 percent per annum. This experience led to a widespread assumption that common stocks provided not only a hedge against inflation but a real net gain over and above inflation: indeed that a little inflation was good for stock prices! Some very smart people projected "more of the same" into the future.

In fact, the level of stock prices in 1980 was at about the level it had been in December 1968. In those 11 years the CPI had risen by 150 percent!

There is little need to drive home the point any further: The conventional practice of projecting economic variables 10 or 12 years into the future on the basis of what happened 10 or 12 years in the past assumes continuity. This practice can be disastrously misleading when we run into discontinuities. An equally serious mistake is to take economic changes that occur within a zone of discontinuity and project these changes into the future by assuming that what we have witnessed is the onset of a new and continuing trend. The danger in the early 1980s is that many people are doing precisely that.

The Geometric Trendists

Analysts who subscribe to the *trend* view of the 1970s and thus a *replay* view for the 1980s are by no means a homogeneous group. There is an entire spectrum of trendists.

At one extreme edge squats a group of those who project the trends geometrically—who believe, literally, that inflation and our other ills will continue to worsen in geometric magnitudes in the 1980s, i.e., that prices and rates in 1990 will be as high relative to those in 1980 as 1980 prices and rates were to those in 1970. The results of carrying out such an exercise are frightening.

Let us begin with the rate of inflation. This rate has been rising in wavelike fashion ever since it started to climb in 1966; each crest has been higher than the preceding crest and the inflation rate at each trough higher than at the one before. The inflation rate was 1.5 percent prior to 1965, 3 percent in 1966, 6 percent in 1970, 12 percent in 1974, 18 percent in the first quarter of 1980. For the geometric trendists the obvious conclusion is, "Look out, here comes 30 percent inflation and 30 percent interest rates on the next inevitable wave a few years down the road." Where does it all end? To use the vivid prose geometric trendists prefer, it ends in a "cataclysmic economic collapse."

The geometric projections implied for the price of oil and gold are even more startling. Oil prices rose by a factor of 18 during the 1970s; in a replay scenario the price would rocket from $36 a barrel at year-end 1980 to around $650 a barrel by 1990. As for the price of gold, the geometric trend projection for 1990 is between $6,000 and a staggering $10,000 an ounce! It is enough to make one head for the hills with all of one's assets in a sack or two of Krugerrands, a ton of dehydrated food, and a survival manual.

A lot of people believe that such a scenario is not only possible but probable. Indeed doomsaying had become one of the leading "growth" industries by 1980. For as little as $11.95 or as much as $1,000 the public has been buying access in record volume to books, tapes, newsletters, and one-day seminars. The haruspices of Rome never had it so good.

In spite of the huge audiences it commands, the geometric progression scenario for prices and rates in 1990 is not a likely one. If in the early years of the 1980s the economy does move along the path it has been on since 1970, one thing we can be sure of is that it *cannot* continue on such a track to 1990. Long before that, perhaps in the unpropitious year 1984, the financial system will collapse and with it the essentially free-market system as we now know it. But interpreted in one special sense the basic message of the doomsayers has a large grain of truth in it: If we do not take incisive policy actions to disinflate now in an orderly way, we will be forced to disinflate in a highly disorderly way within five years.

The Moderate Trendists

The mainstream of those forecasters who believe that we are caught inexorably in a continuing trend of high inflation and rising energy prices projects a scenario for the 1980s that is far less violent than the one just outlined. But it is nonetheless darkly pessimistic.

In their view, the U.S. is now stuck with a high embedded or built-in rate of inflation even if we exclude the added impact from random shocks caused by large leaps in oil prices or farm prices or the after-effects of periodic devaluations. The so-called embedded rate of inflation is equal to the difference between the average annual rate of increase in wages and fringe benefits per hour and any offsetting increase in productivity (output per hour of work). By 1980 the embedded inflation rate had risen to around 11 percent per annum. For this rate to fall, either one or both of two things must happen: Labor's demand for increased wages and fringes (such as cost-of-living adjustments) has to fall, or the average annual improvement in productivity has to rise. Given the recent record on inflation plus the fact that most people who receive their income from the government are protected against inflation (their salaries and benefits are indexed to the CPI), it is not likely that private-sector demand for increased wages and fringes will fall. Given the progressive worsening we have had in the rate of productivity gains (which averaged less than 0.5 percent a year between 1973 and 1980), it is even less likely that we will witness a sudden new leap in average productivity in the 1980s. In short, the U.S. is likely to be stuck with a basic inflation rate of above 10 percent a year as future increases in wages and prices chase each other in joint orbit.

To this basic inflation rate we have to add the extra push that will come from further jumps in the price of oil (the moderate trendists expect this pattern to continue) and jumps in import prices each time the exchange rate of the U.S. dollar declines against the currencies of the better-behaved economies, such as Japan and West Germany (they expect this 1970s trend to continue too).

Thus, the moderate trendists' forecast is that inflation will rise by 10 to 12 percent in "good years" with gusts up to 20 percent depending on what OPEC does to the price of oil and what nature does to harvests.

The moderate trendists believe that government policies in the 1980s will generally follow the trend we witnessed during the 1970s—vacillating between temporary concern over inflation every time it accelerates to a new high and concern for a host of other political priorities such as unemployment and social programs every time they appear to need attention, even at the cost of risking further increases in the inflation rate. The idea that government might be capable of pursuing a sustained and single-minded set of policies designed to wring out inflation is ruled out on the grounds that it would be politically infeasible: The political pain of unemployment and economic slack would be too high a price for a populist democracy to pay.

If their projected scenario for inflation is right, the U.S. Consumer Price Index (1967 = 100) will climb to between 750 and 800 by 1990. By then every dollar you or I put into a dollar-denominated security (such as a long-term bond) back in 1967 will be worth one-half of two bits!

The implied forecast for the price of oil is that it will rise faster than the U.S. inflation rate. The OPEC oil ministers who determine or try to determine OPEC's long-range pricing policy agree with this forecast: Their "formula" for oil prices in the 1980s is for a *real* increase equal to the real growth rate of the main importing countries, estimated to be between 3 and 4 percent a year. Adding this to the expected U.S. inflation rate one gets a projection of oil prices rising *at least* 15 percent a year—"at least" because the formula given above is what the so-called pricing doves such as Saudi Arabia espouse. The pricing hawks—Libya, Algeria, and Iran—demonstrated all through the 1970s that they want (and can frequently get) a much faster rate of price escalation. Even at a 15 percent rate, the price of petroleum would rise to $130 a barrel by 1990 or $3.10 per U.S. gallon just for the crude!

As for gold, it is clear that anybody who bought or held gold in 1980 at around $650 per ounce must have been expecting the dollar price of gold to rise by at least 13 percent a year, because that was the rate available on long-term U.S. Treasury bonds. At 13 percent a year the implied projection for the price of gold by 1990 is $3,395 an ounce!

Adapting to the Future

Can our economic and financial system take another decade of even such a "moderate" replay scenario? The answer is, no. People learn from experience. Once they start learning to expect inflation, as they clearly had by 1980, they adapt their behavior to these expectations extremely rapidly. The adaptations can take place in many ways, all of them rational from the point of view of the individual but eventually destructive for the system as a whole. Our system of private voluntary

"Take it from me, Harlow, things are going to get a lot worse before they get better."

saving, progressive income taxes, and long-term capital markets was not designed to coexist with serious inflation.

The rate of inflation expected in the moderate replay scenario—10 or 12 percent a year for the decade ahead, even if new oil shocks can be avoided—is more severe than we experienced in the 1970s. But there are other, more important differences between the situation in 1981 as compared to 1971.

One crucial difference is that in 1971 there were no widespread expectations that the then current rate of 5 percent inflation would persist—let alone worsen—and hence no widespread attempts by individuals to protect themselves by cutting down on their saving and increasing their borrowing. By 1981 both expectations and behavior had changed: In 1971 people saved 8 percent out of their disposable income; in early 1981 this figure was down to less than 5 percent, in spite of the fact that in the interim there had been a large increase in the amount of saving going into contractually mandated pension, annuity, and insurance plans. Indeed in early 1981 purely "voluntary" (i.e., noncontractual) saving by households was around zero. Also in the interim, people's propensity to borrow had risen markedly: In 1979 they borrowed $212 billion or 13 percent of their disposable income compared to $34 billion or 5 percent in 1970. As expectations of continued inflation spread and harden, these two trends will continue. People will save less and less, borrow more and more, and in the process soon bring on an even higher rate of inflation than the 10 to 12 percent now expected for the decade in the moderate replay scenario.

There is an even deeper problem to be faced. By definition, households, business, and government collectively comprise the entire U.S. economy. If households as a group are driven by their expectations to become net borrowers, if the business sector continues to be a net borrower (which it *must* be in order to expand our stock of productive plant and equipment), and if the government remains a net borrower (in order to finance its habitual deficits), one has to ask: Where is the lending coming from to fund all this net borrowing? There are only two sources.

One source is for the government to "print"* enough new money to satisfy the demands of borrowers. Almost everybody agrees that such expansion of the money supply leads rapidly to an acceleration in the inflation rate. In short, if this is the solution adopted, the moderate

---

*The actual process we use to create new money is far more subtle than mere "printing" but amounts to exactly the same thing in the end (see Chapter 3).

replay scenario will soon escalate into the kind of disastrous geometric trend scenario that the rival doomsayers envisage.

The second source that can satisfy a net U.S. demand for borrowing is for us to sell or mortgage our assets to foreigners. Such a process could go on for a long time, many decades in fact, because we have a lot of assets to sell or mortgage: farms and homes and companies whose total value already runs to many trillions of 1980 dollars. Mortgage or sale of U.S. assets to foreign interests is a better solution to the problem than is that offered by the device of money printing, in the sense that the former can go on for longer. The real issue is whether it offers a better solution than that available through a set of policies that eradicates inflation itself, the principal cause of our original dilemma.

The ways in which individuals respond to high rates of expected inflation by shifting their saving/borrowing/spending habits relative to their current income is only one form of rational adaptive behavior. They can also shift the form in which they hold their accumulations of past savings.

At year-end 1980 we held some $1.3 trillion dollars of our *past* savings in nonbank thrift institutions such as savings and loan associations ($622 billion), life insurance companies ($467 billion), mutual savings banks ($169 billion), and credit unions ($65 billion). In turn, these institutions have lent out the bulk of these funds largely in the form of long-term fixed-rate loans (secured by mortgages and bonds) that provide the very lifeblood of a system of private capitalism and private home ownership.

Such a system—in which individuals lend to institutions at a fixed rate (but subject to withdrawal either directly from deposit accounts or through policy loans at life insurance companies) and these institutions in turn lend to business, government, and other individuals on a long-term basis at fixed rates—works extremely well until inflation enters the picture. When inflation accelerates and expectations of future inflation become widespread, market rates of interest rise in order to offset the loss in purchasing power that all lenders must suffer who lend *today's* dollar and much later get back dollars of diminished purchasing power.

When market rates of interest rise because the inflation rate itself is rising, depositors (or in the case of life insurance companies, policy holders) remove their past savings from thrift institutions in order to reinvest at the more lucrative rates the current market is offering. The thrift institutions face two choices, both dangerous.

First, they can try to hold onto these funds by themselves offering individuals rates of return as high as the open market offers. There are two problems with respect to this line of defense. One is that governmental regulation with respect to interest-rate ceilings does not allow them the freedom to compete head-on with open-market rates. The other is that even if the thrift institutions could compete, they would soon find that their average cost of funds (the rate they pay their depositors) will rise *above* the average rate they are earning on all the bonds and mortgages they themselves acquired in prior periods when interest rates were much lower. As their average borrowing rate rises above their average lending rate, they will begin to suffer losses each year. If rates remain high year after year, such accumulating losses will eventually drive them toward insolvency.

The second choice they face is no better. If institutions allow their depositors to withdraw funds by not offering competitive interest rates, they will have to liquidate assets in order to fund the withdrawals. A 30-year 8 percent mortgage or bond with 20 years to go before maturity that is liquidated in a world of 16 percent mortgage rates or bond rates will command a market price of about 60 cents on each dollar—selling these assets at market value will lead inexorably to insolvency because depositors have the right to be paid 100 cents on each dollar.

The vulnerability of the thrift institutions to high or rising inflation and interest rates was much greater in 1981 than it had been ten years earlier. The American public had become far more interest-rate conscious and hence far more willing to shift their financial assets to forms that offered better protection against further erosion. The 1970s had also spawned a large number of convenient vehicles into which the population could readily move their past accumulated savings—money-market funds (which in early 1981 were growing at the rate of 10 percent a month), gold and other precious metals, real estate, Eurodollars, commodities, and even such investments as precious stones and antiques.

The world envisaged by the moderate trendists, a world of 10 to 12 percent inflation and 12 to 15 percent interest rates, simply cannot go on for another decade without a major breakdown of the financial institutions in which the U.S. population holds such a large portion of their savings. At a 12 percent inflation rate, even the 1980 dollar, already vastly depreciated from its past purchasing power, would lose a further 70 percent of its value by 1990. Long before that occurs, major segments of the financial system would be insolvent.

The Role of Policy

The two versions of the replay scenario for the 1980s differ from one another in significant respects, but they also share many elements of similarity. Before continuing, it is useful to summarize the similarities and differences between what each appears to be saying.

In the first place the leading exponents of the two trendist views belong in two quite distinct groups. The geometric trendists, as I have dubbed them, are characteristically financial market people, generally commercially oriented and frequently flamboyantly visible. By contrast, the moderate trendists are generally serious professional economists, many of whom have had substantial experience in government.

A critical difference between the two groups concerns the role that policy can or might play in shaping the future. According to the geometric trendists, it is already too late for policy actions to have much effect on the future because the momentum of accelerating inflation is already too strong for any counteraction to be effective. Their conclusion is that some sort of serious financial collapse will occur before the government can be forced to step in with action drastic enough to put the pieces together again. Their concern is to protect their clients from the consequences of the collapse itself. The general formula is to advise that smart people should now shift all or part of their wealth out of dollar-denominated claims before the impending collapse becomes so obvious that everybody else tries to do so, a move that will trigger the collapse itself.

The moderate trendists do not share this nihilistic view that policy changes are futile. What they say is that it is too late for *traditional* monetary and fiscal policies to work efficiently in a free-market setting: Such policies will take too long, involve enormous costs to society in unemployment and lost output, and furthermore breach our sense of equity too flagrantly to be worth trying. They maintain that inflation is now firmly embedded in the system at around 10 to 12 percent a year, and patterns of free-market behavior based on these expectations can serve only to worsen this rate. For the majority of the moderate trendists, the only workable solution is for the U.S. to abandon the market system at least temporarily and replace it with a system based on command and control from Washington, namely control over one or more of the following: wages, prices, interest rates, the allocation of credit, and foreign exchange.

In spite of major differences, the two wings of the trendist view are in agreement about one thing: The inflationary trend of the 1970s cannot be reversed in an orderly way; so long as large segments of society are left free to choose their behavior, financial performance will worsen until one of two things happens—either the system itself collapses or the government imposes strict controls over wages, prices, and other dimensions of economic life. Neither group offers a diagnosis that can be described as cheerful. Fortunately, there is a third school of thought that is less dour.

"Nervous, Kid?"

Drawing by Chick Larsen
Courtesy *Richmond* (Va.) *Times-Dispatch*

2

The 1970s as a Watershed

GEOGRAPHERS USE THE WORD WATERSHED in two ways. The first and preferred usage refers to the entire drainage area of a major river system;
the second refers to the zone that divides two major river systems from
one another. Watershed in the title of the present chapter is used in the
second sense. There are watersheds in history akin to those in geographic space—identifiable zones of discontinuity or transition that divide the centuries into understandable segments. On one side of these
watersheds the flow of economic events, indeed of ideas, is in one
predominant and predictable direction; on the other side the flows both
of events and ideas point elsewhere. Within the watershed itself, the
flows are often turbulent and their ultimate direction cannot be discerned.

So far as recent economic history is concerned, there is almost complete agreement that one long-term trend remarkable for both growth
and stability began around 1946 and ended in the early 1970s. The disagreement is over how we should interpret the course of events since
then. For some observers, notably the trendists discussed in the previous chapter, the decade just past represents the beginning of a new
long-term trend. For others, the 1970s represent an extended watershed
between two long-term trends, one that ended in the early 1970s and
another about to begin in the early 1980s as perceptions, politics, and
policies precipitate a turning point in events. The shape of the economic

future in the 1980s and beyond depends crucially on which of these interpretations of the recent past is correct.

Unfortunately history can provide clues but no unequivocal answers to this question. In the vicinity of a watershed she always leaves us guessing. Moreover, the historical record for modern industrial economies covers no more than three or four such watershed episodes, two of which were associated with global wars. Nonetheless these long-term trends and the intervening watersheds deserve our attention.

Historical Watersheds

Although the Industrial Revolution and modern economic thought began in England some 200 years ago, what we now call modern industrial capitalism—the age of mass production for mass consumption—really began in the U.S., around 1890. The years surrounding that date comprise a watershed in U.S. economic and financial history. For some 25 years prior to that watershed U.S. prices and interest rates had been falling; they bottomed out in the early 1890s and then began a long and steady rise that lasted a quarter century. In the economy itself there was a huge burst of invention, most of which had major economic implications and which ushered in the age of steel and oil.

The period from 1913 to 1920 around World War I marked another major watershed. The course of economic events for two decades after that war differed in significant ways from what had taken place during the two decades prior to 1913. The prewar decades were characterized by rapid economic growth, stable exchange rates, gently rising prices and interest rates, and the firm establishment of a system of industrialized market economies in Europe, North America, and Japan. It was, as the French put it, a *belle epoque*. After 1920, the pace of economic growth abated markedly, especially in Europe; prices and interest rates declined; the spread of the market system to new nations came to a halt; international exchange-rate stability and trade deteriorated rapidly. Finally, during the 1930s, the entire market system itself was on the verge of an almost total collapse. It was a stagnant world marked by massive unemployment and distress. Many observers, forecasting a long-run continuation of economic stagnancy and disarray, were ready to see the system buried. All of these doomsday forecasts turned out to be quite wrong, for we entered another major watershed at the onset of World War II. The war itself (1939–45) constituted a third important turning point in the course of economic events.

After World War II, the market system not only survived, it was launched into a quarter century of unprecedented economic growth and prosperity. From 1948 to 1973, productivity per man-hour in the industrial market economies rose at twice the annual rate experienced during the preceding 75 years; so, therefore, did standards of living. The rate and steadiness of economic growth of the market economies had declined, and in Western Europe it had shrunk almost to zero between 1919 and 1939. After 1948 growth accelerated again to reach levels far above those achieved even during the so-called golden age prior to World War I. International financial stability and the stability of exchange rates among the major nations, both of which had collapsed during the 1930s, were fully restored by 1949 and were maintained for 20 years. Trade and exchange among nations grew even faster than the individual economies themselves. The scope of the industrial market system itself expanded to bring in a significant number of new members whose economies flourished: South Korea, Taiwan, Hong Kong, Singapore, and Malaysia on the Pacific rim; Brazil and Mexico in the west; and Spain, Greece, and Turkey on the southern fringe of Europe.

Given such resounding success, why and how did the postwar period come to an end in the early 1970s? According to some observers, prosperity itself sowed the seeds of its own eventual destruction. There is considerable merit to this diagnosis. Prosperity leads governments to try to do more and more of the things that generate political popularity, such as a redistribution of income, increased social services and benefits, and greater regulation of industry. These ultimately erode the sources from which prosperity itself flows because they inevitably dampen the net economic rewards offered for business success and reduce the net economic penalty for failure; i.e., they destroy the link between work and consumption that lies at the heart of a pure market system. There is ample evidence that such developments took place in the United States and Europe. In the same way, an increasing tendency to flirt with a little inflation through budget deficits and easy money policies in the interest of pushing the pace of growth and income redistribution inexorably leads to accelerating inflation. Clearly, this set of forces was also at work in the late 1960s and early 1970s. But such long-run forces do not in themselves lead to a critical turning point *in all the major industrial economies at the same time.* Something more is needed to complete the explanation of why the course of events in the 1970s, especially after the end of 1973, was so markedly different from that during the preceding quarter century. That explanation lies in three major developments that converged that year:

1. The onset of a huge wave of peacetime inflation all over the industrialized world;

2. The 350 percent jump in the price of oil, the system's most important source of energy; and
3. The final collapse of the postwar system of pegged exchange rates among the industrial economies.

The confluence of the three events, and especially the interaction among them, was powerful enough to bring the postwar period to an end.

The Discontinuity in Growth

The clearest evidence that a sharp discontinuity occurred in 1973 is the abrupt slowdown in the rate of industrial growth that occurred in all the major economies after that year. Table 1 shows the average annual rate of industrial growth for ten advanced industrialized economies for the 18-year period prior to 1973 and for the 5-year period between the end of 1973, when the first energy crisis struck, and the end of 1978, before the second energy crisis descended.

Table 1: Growth of Industrial Production
(percent per annum)

	1955–73	1973–78*
United States	4.5	3.0
Japan	13.5	1.0
West Germany	5.8	1.4
France	6.1	0.8
United Kingdom	3.0	0.5
Italy	7.2	0.8
Canada	5.8	2.0
Netherlands	6.8	0.9
Belgium	4.4	0
Switzerland	5.3	−2.5
Average of 9 (excludes U.S.)	6.4	0.5

*From fourth quarter to fourth quarter

There are two especially interesting phenomena reflected in this table:
1. From 1955 to 1973 very rapid rates of annual growth were achieved by all the major market economies: Industrial growth averaged 4.5 percent a year for the United States and 6.4 percent a year for the other nine economies. By contrast, during the five years after 1973, the U.S. growth rate was down to 3 percent and the growth rate of the other nine had fallen even more sharply—to less than 1 percent per annum.

2. Prior to 1973, the United States was among the slowest growing of the ten economies. For the five-year period after 1973, the U.S. emerged with the fastest rate of industrial growth. The Swiss economy had actually begun to shrink.

Both phenomena deserve an explanation. It is useful to do so by first examining the effect that the events of 1973 had on the capacity of economies to grow.

The Energy Effect

Energy is a major input into the production process of modern industrial economies. To express the matter in somewhat oversimplified terms, the very rapid growth rates achieved prior to 1973 were heavily based on one central idea: the substitution of energy for human sweat, via installed machinery and equipment. The process worked well so long as energy itself was plentiful and cheap relative to human time. We economized on one factor of production—people—by using another factor—energy—in larger and larger relative amounts. Prior to 1973, the real price of energy was falling relative to wage rates. Thus, the use of energy and energy-using equipment relative to labor rose, and this in turn gave us the strong and steady rise in productivity per man-hour we enjoyed.

In 1973–74, and even more clearly in 1979–80, the postwar assumption of plentiful and relatively inexpensive energy had to be replaced by the opposite assumption: Over the next decade at least, energy will be scarce and relatively expensive. How then do we achieve ever-increasing output per man-hour with our present technology? The answer is that we cannot. The industrial economies, or at least their industrial sectors, will have to adjust to a much lower capacity to grow during most of the 1980s than we enjoyed prior to 1973. Such a slowdown is already occurring, as Table 1 shows.

Industrial output—generally defined as the output of a nation's factories, mines, and utilities—is of course only part of total economic output. The remaining portion of a nation's GNP consists of the value added by the trade, services, and governmental sectors of the economy. These sectors are less energy-intensive than is industry. Prior to 1973, industrial production for each of the countries shown in Table 1 rose more rapidly than did their total GNP. By contrast, since 1973, the GNP in these countries has risen significantly faster than has the paltry growth in their industrial production—another indication that the quantum leap in energy prices was indeed a critical factor in the change that has occurred since the end of 1973.

The Inflation Effect

A second major change since 1973—the onset of very high rates of inflation—also had an impact on the capacity of economies to grow. The effects of inflation are not neutral, especially in a country such as the U.S. which depends heavily on a progressive income tax and which uses an accounting system based on "original costs." The combination of high rates of inflation and high marginal tax rates* reduces the ability and willingness of both corporations and individuals to save.

The untaxed funds corporations are allowed to set aside for the purpose of replacing the stock of their productive capital (known as depreciation allowances) become increasingly inadequate as price levels rise. Just in order to *maintain* the stock of productive capital, these inadequate depreciation allowances have to be supplemented by new funds that must somehow be obtained either from earnings or from the capital markets. To make matters worse, the flow of earnings itself is subject to an increasing rate of taxation. Thus, in the U.S. system, inflation levies a large tax on capital.

As for individuals, the incentive to save is seriously eroded when inflation rates rise. Take, for example, the record 18 percent rate of inflation that prevailed between December 1979 and March 1980. Interest rates were also at record highs during this period. The interest rate on six-month Treasury bills reached an unprecedented level of 14 percent in early 1980. This key rate determines all other short-term rates in the U.S., including the rate of interest that banks, savings and loans, and other thrift institutions can offer on the popular six-month money-market certificates for deposits between $10,000 and $100,000, a rate that is set each week at the Treasury bill rate *plus* ½ percent. But this reward to savers is taxable at each individual's marginal tax bracket. For most savers, the *marginal* tax rate (including federal, state, and local income taxes) was around 40 percent. For the richest savers, the rate of taxation on interest—which is defined as "unearned income"—ran as high as 75 percent. The apparently high 14 percent yield on Treasury bills was thus reduced by taxation to 8½ percent for the average saver and to a meager 3½ percent for those in the top tax brackets. After allowing for the effects of inflation on the dollars that the saver gets back, the *real* aftertax rate of return in early 1980—adjusted for the large fall in the purchasing

*Economists use the word *marginal* to mean incremental. In this context it refers to the rate of tax that is applied by the Internal Revenue Service against the last $100 earned in a given calendar year. For example, a married couple with one child who earn $20,000 will owe $2,710 in federal taxes. Their *average* tax rate is about 13½ percent. If they had earned $26,660 by working overtime their tax bill would have risen to $4,245. Their marginal tax is equal to the *increase* in tax per extra dollar earned. In this case it is the *additional* tax of $1,534 they had to pay on the *additional* income of $6,660. The *marginal* rate is 23 percent.

"SEE YOUR RAISE AND RAISE YOU BACK"

Drawing by Herblock
© 1979 Herblock in *The Washington Post*

power of the dollar—was therefore a *negative* 9½ percent for the average saver and a *negative* 14½ percent for the individual in the top tax bracket. This is what we mean by the phrase "beating the saver over the head."

It is thus no wonder that the rate of saving by individuals in the United States fell to extremely low levels by the end of the 1970s in spite of the illusion created by high nominal interest rates. Because the measured rate of saving includes *contractual* saving through contributions to insurance and retirement programs, that very low rate of total saving actually meant that *voluntary* saving was close to zero. Collectively, the United States, the richest nation in the world, had been induced into consuming nearly 100 percent of the net output it produced.

Productivity and Living Standards

Saving performs a critical function in the growth of our average per capita living standards. A zero rate of saving means that society as a whole is consuming all it produces each year. This leaves no resources that can be used for the purpose of expanding that society's stock of productive capital (plant, equipment, and machines). Although some increase in average output per hour of work is technically possible without any increase in the stock of capital, the bulk of past increases has required a larger and better capital stock associated with each worker. To put it in simple terms, one man sitting in the air-conditioned cab of a giant coal-cutting machine can produce more coal in comfort in one day than his identical twin can produce with a pickax in a year of grimy toil. Without increases in the capital stock per worker, productivity per hour of work is unlikely to rise. Why is this of consequence? Because rising productivity per hour of work is the *only* enduring source of rising economic standards of living for a nation. Without saving and investment we cannot increase our per capita standard of living.

Although a positive rate of saving is one necessary condition for productivity growth, it is not in itself a sufficient condition. Somebody has to borrow or otherwise rent the funds that are saved and convert them into investments in new technologies and new capital goods, a process that involves skill and risk and therefore one that requires the prospect of a rate of return over and above the rate that has to be paid to the saver to persuade him to save and lend rather than spend. In short, our material progress requires an environment in which both of two conditions are satisfied: The net aftertax, after-inflation reward to the saver must be large enough to overcome his natural inclination to spend all he earns; the net aftertax, after-inflation reward to the risk taker who converts that saving into productive capital must also be large enough to overcome his natural aversion to risk.

During the 1970s it was clear that the U.S. government, which has a large say in creating or destroying both these essential conditions, was doing more to destroy than to create. One result is that for four years, from 1976 to 1980, average output per hour of work in the United States showed no rise. For the entire seven-year period after 1973, output per *employed* person rose at only about one-tenth of 1 percent per annum. At that rate it will take nearly 500 years to achieve another doubling of each worker's standard of living even if we assume that there will be no further diversions of income from workers to nonworkers in society. Contrast that with the situation prior to 1973 when output per person employed had almost doubled in 25 years.

From the point of view of those who produce our output, the actual results achieved between 1973 and 1980 were even poorer than those just outlined. Those who do the producing do not get to keep all the output they produce, nor even a constant fraction of that output. By enlarging their own share in total output, governments here and abroad took away much more than the trivial gain in per worker output that we achieved between 1973 and 1980. This left the average worker absolutely worse off in 1980 than his counterparts had been seven years earlier.

The OPEC nations, through huge increases in the price of oil, increased their take from us by about 2½ percent of total U.S. output, thus leaving us 2½ percent less for ourselves. This act of taxation without representation was of course well publicized by our government. What was not publicized was that the share of GNP taken through taxation by our own elected federal government also increased by approximately the same amount—2½ percent of total output. The result was that real economic output per employed worker available for each average worker fell by almost 5 percent between 1973 and 1980. If that trend is allowed to continue, output available to each average U.S. worker will regress by the end of the century to the level that the average American worker had attained in the early 1950s.

The Policy Dimension

Turning points in the flow of economic and financial events rarely occur without corresponding movements in the flow of ideas and in the thrust of policies that are influenced by ideas. Sometimes events lead ideas; sometimes it is the other way around. In either case they reinforce one another. The success that the industrial world enjoyed during the postwar period was not the simple result of good fortune. It was in large part the result of two ideas developed in the late 1930s before World War II erupted.

The first of these ideas, now clearly associated with the name of the British economist John Maynard Keynes, was that in some situations a market economy left to itself might generate insufficient aggregate demand to maintain its human and industrial capacity at a reasonable level of full employment. In such conditions it was a proper duty and responsibility of government to correct matters by creating an addition to aggregate demand sufficient to reabsorb unemployed resources. It could achieve this objective by increasing spending (without raising taxes) or by cutting taxes (without reducing spending) or by both methods—in short, by deliberately running a federal deficit.

The second idea was that the policies associated with the miserable performance of the interwar period, especially the terrible decade of the 1930s, were sterile and should be reversed. These counterproductive policies included protective tariffs, floating exchange rates, competitive devaluations, exchange controls, and futile attempts to balance budgets by tax-rate increases.

After World War II ended, these two new ideas became the foundation for a new set of policies, which in turn led to the huge economic successes we enjoyed for nearly 25 years. One by one, postwar governments adopted "full-employment" policies, i.e., policies that were designed to generate sufficient total demand to keep almost everybody who wanted to work at work. The result was a steady and rapid growth in all the major economies.

On the international front the self-defeating attempts by each nation to gain at the expense of its trading partners (through tariffs, exchange devaluations, and the like) were replaced by organized multinational cooperation. The Bretton Woods agreements reestablished a system of stable exchange rates for the major countries as each pegged the value of its currency to the U.S. dollar. The General Agreement on Trade and Tariffs (GATT) led to a steady lowering of trade barriers and tariffs. As a result, after World War II trade among nations grew even faster than the average growth in the free world's output.

Gradually at first and then more rapidly as time passed, the fresh new postwar ideas were pushed to illogical extremes. The sensible Keynesian idea that in addition to supply power, aggregate demand was *also* important to keep an economy healthy was replaced by the senseless idea that virtually any increase in aggregate demand was a good thing. The sensible idea that supply power alone was not a sufficient condition for economic growth was replaced by the senseless idea that supply power could be taken for granted. The idea that full employment was a legitimate goal of national economic policy was replaced by the senseless idea that the achievement of a low unemployment rate was the only objective of economic policy.

By the mid-1960s the Congress of the United States began to believe that the basic economic problem of mankind—the capacity to supply goods and services—had been solved. It then began to concentrate its attention on the politically popular issues of social and environmental reform, without any careful regard for how these changes might harm the ability of the private sector to attend to the supply side.

Much of the legislation that Congress decreed in the 1960s and 1970s had important economic side effects; some were good but they were mainly adverse. Collectively, the legislation and regulation that followed induced large counterproductive shifts in income, wealth, power, and the way we use our human energies. The principal shifts were from the private sector to the government, from the economy to the environment, from the producer to the consumer, from the states and cities to Washington, from the young to the old, from the decision maker to the bureaucrat, and from the output of useful commodities to the output of compliance reports and legal briefs. A huge outpouring of federal regulations was engineered with no serious consideration given to the detrimental effects it might have on more fundamental economic objectives whose steady attainment is essential to the general welfare of the nation itself—reasonable price stability, the integrity of the dollar, a steady rise in productivity, the balance of energy supply and demand, the vitality of our industrial plants. By 1980 we had achieved a number of commendable objectives—but at the cost of losing some that are essential. The objectives we neglected for 15 years suddenly surfaced as major problems. In the 1980s they will require more than *some* attention—they will require *priority* attention.

Many sensible people now believe that the game of modern politics will not allow for any such reordering of priorities. But they misread the countercurrents that have been showing up in recent history. In mid-1980 only one major U.S. presidential contender recited the liberal litany of the 1960s; he captured some hearts but not his party's nomination. The election of 1980 was won on the basis of fundamental economic issues—the winners were those who advocated a return of policy to its older emphases on the supply side of the national economic equation—work, thrift, smaller government, lower tax rates, and a larger reliance on market forces.

The necessary shift in policies that is required to achieve these now newer priorities will not be accomplished easily. Economic ideas are easy to implement only when they flow in tandem with social and demographic tides. That is why the Keynesian revolution in economic thinking caught on so well in the 1950s and 1960s. That revolution called for increased emphasis on aggregate demand, i.e., more government spending, a larger public sector, a larger redistribution of wealth and income through taxation, more borrowing and less saving, a larger bias in favor of the consumer as opposed to the producer. All of these were politically easy to achieve.

By contrast, what is now being dubbed as the supply-side revolution of 1981 requires an opposite set of policies: less consumption and more saving, less government, less redistribution from workers to nonworkers, less bias in favor of consumers relative to producers. In short, it requires an incisive set of actions designed to correct the three problems that brought the superior economic performance of the postwar period to a close in 1973: too much inflation, too great a dependence on imported oil, and too much government. The real clues to the shape of the 1980s lie in the answer to two questions:

1. Will the government alter its policies as radically as the situation requires?
2. Will an alteration in policies achieve enough success on all three fronts to more than offset whatever short-run pains it might cause?

If the answer to both questions is affirmative, a replay of the 1970s is the least likely scenario for the decade ahead. But we do not have a final answer to even the first question. All we have is considerable evidence that the U.S. has dragged itself, slowly and reluctantly at first but nonetheless with increasing momentum, toward the necessary alterations in policies called for by the new situation that the U.S. and most of the industrial world has confronted since 1973.

Traumas of the Mid-Seventies

The traumas of 1973–74 had a big impact on the capacity of the industrial nations to grow. They had a slower, but eventually larger impact on the way nations conducted their economic policies. The Swiss, who quickly understood that the integrity of their currency was a more lucrative asset than the number of visitors to Zermatt, had already switched to anti-inflationary policies long before the oil crisis struck. In 1973 they had brought their money supply into tight control. The Japanese, with their flair for national common sense, reacted swiftly and sensibly to the change imposed by inflation and very expensive oil. For example, they mothballed a large fraction of their fuel-inefficient aluminum facilities, and they redeployed their large supply of human energy into producing even more fuel-efficient cars and superefficient microprocessors.

Other nations, one by one, fell into line with the new realities. The biggest and most important industrial economy was the last large nation to recognize that something fundamental had happened: The United States, unable to disentangle itself from the policy mode in which it had cemented itself in the late 1960s, finally began to see the light only as the 1970s were ending.

During the 1950s and 1960s, the willingness and ability of governments to pursue expansive monetary, fiscal, and foreign-exchange policies was one major reason for the sustained and rapid growth that the free world enjoyed prior to 1973. In the post-1973 world of high inflation, high oil prices, floating exchange rates, and the large balance-of-trade deficits caused by oil imports, both the willingness and freedom of most governments to pursue expansionary policies were seriously curtailed. The reason is simple: The huge jump in oil prices inevitably led to a huge trading-account surplus for the oil-exporting countries. The counterpart of their surplus was a huge deficit for the rest of the world. Such deficits weaken the exchange rate of a nation's currency, especially in the floating world in which market forces drive exchange rates. In turn, any decline in a nation's exchange rate relative to the U.S. dollar brings an immediate increase in the cost of imported oil (which was fixed in terms of U.S. dollars) as well as of other imports. This worsens the inflation rate for that nation, which in turn weakens the currency even further, leading to a vicious spiral that can be stopped only by pursuing a less expansionary policy.

The existence of these potential hazards created a dilemma for those who direct national economic policies. The dilemma showed up quite clearly at the end of 1976. The sharp worldwide contraction of economic activity that began at the end of 1973 reached its trough by mid-1975. Thereafter, industrial output in most nations bounced back spontaneously and rapidly, until by year-end 1976 output in most economies was about back to the prerecession levels of 1973. However, around the end of 1976, the rate of expansion in all countries began to slow markedly.

Three years of zero net growth in the context of a rising labor force and some rise in productivity had left unemployment rates in all countries at very high levels relative to unemployment rates experienced prior to 1973. As growth began to slow at the end of 1976 these politically sensitive unemployment rates showed signs of rising again. Prior to 1973, there would have been little doubt about what had to be done. Every government would have provided enough stimulus through fiscal and monetary policies to accelerate growth rates in order to bring unemployment down to acceptable levels. But in the post-1973 world, curing unemployment could no longer be given the unequivocal priority it once had. There were now other priorities:

1. Although inflation rates were down from the extremely high levels of 1974, they were still high and the threat that they would accelerate again was a problem most governments could not ignore.

2. The free world's huge trading deficit with the oil-exporting countries was also down from the peak rate of $65 billion a year reached in 1974, but it was still very large. To maintain access to credit markets in order to finance these deficits, most countries had to make a visible effort to minimize deficits in their other trading balances.

3. Because the world was now on a system of floating exchange rates, governments had to be concerned with the ever-present threat of a fall in exchange rates and the severe impact which that could have on their internal inflation.

International Reactions to the Post-1973 World

Most nations reacted predictably to the new realities and adopted policies designed to keep inflation down and growth slow even at the cost of high or rising unemployment rates. Some nations, notably Switzerland and West Germany, adopted slow-growth policies voluntarily. They did not have to do so, for their currencies were basically strong. They did so because they assigned an extremely high priority to the objective of wringing out the unacceptable rates of inflation they had suffered. The West German willingness to step on the policy brakes reflects Germany's disastrous experience with inflation in the 1920s. As far as Switzerland is concerned, the story goes that she not only stepped on the brakes, but drove the truck into a wall; fortunately for the Swiss, an Italian was sitting in the front seat. This refers to the fact that a sizeable portion of Swiss employment in 1973 consisted of Italian workers. As the economy switched from the path of rapid industrial growth that had been experienced prior to 1973 to an actual shrinkage of industrial output after 1973, the first to be disemployed were the Italian guest workers.

Both West Germany and Switzerland achieved a rapid decline in the experienced rate of inflation. In West Germany, where inflation had fallen from 6.5 percent in 1974 to 3.8 percent in 1976, the rate continued to fall to 2.4 percent by the end of 1978. Switzerland was even more successful. From nearly 9 percent in 1974, inflation fell to about 0.5 percent by year-end 1978.

Other countries were forced to adopt slow-growth policies even though their natural inclinations might have been to press for high employment and rapid expansion. What forced them to slow down was the brute fact that they would otherwise have to finance their trading deficits by borrowing funds in the international money markets. For example, the United Kingdom got into serious trouble in 1976. The pound slipped rapidly in the exchange markets as trading deficits mounted. In order to borrow the vast sums she needed, the U.K. had to agree to adopt monetary and fiscal policies that would slow both her high rate of inflation and her high rate of imports.

U.S. Reactions to the Post-1973 World

The United States was the outstanding exception to the general rule of a slow-growth policy, particularly during 1977 and 1978. During its first two years, the Carter administration pressed hard for accelerated growth and lower unemployment rates without too much regard for other economic priorities. As a result, in 1977 and 1978 the U.S., which had been one of the slowest-growing industrial economies prior to 1973, experienced the fastest growth in employment and industrial production among the major industrial nations. The policies also explain why the U.S., which had the lowest rate of price inflation prior to 1973, generated one of the highest rates of inflation within the advanced economies by the end of 1978; and, finally, why the U.S. dollar, which had been the world's strongest currency over most of the postwar period, experienced a serious sinking spell all through 1977 and 1978.

Why did the U.S. behave so differently in 1977 and 1978? In the first place there was a difference in national priorities. Unlike West Germany, France, and the U.K., we were unwilling to accept the quantum jump in our unemployment rate that a policy of slow growth implied (for example, the West German unemployment rate in 1978 was four times as high as it had been in 1973). Thus, when Mr. Carter was elected alongside an overwhelmingly Democratic Congress, policy reverted to the instinctual objective of getting the unemployment rate down.

But priorities explain only part of the thrust of our policies in 1977 and 1978. The larger explanation is that the U.S. enjoyed a unique position among nations which allowed it to pursue expansionary policies without immediately having to suffer the adverse consequences that other nations would have suffered had they tried to do the same thing:

1. The price of oil was denominated in U.S. dollars. Thus, a fall in the value of the dollar against the West German mark or the Swiss franc did not inflict on us any immediate rise in the price we paid for heating oil or gasoline. We could therefore ignore, at least temporarily, the complication of having to worry about the impact of our policies on the

". . . And so, as the dollar sinks slowly in the west,
we say farewell . . ."

Drawing by Ray Osrin
© 1978 *Cleveland Plain Dealer*

exchange rate of the dollar. Indeed, when the policies we were pursuing led to a sharp decline in the foreign exchange value of the dollar against other major currencies starting in 1977, the then secretary of the Treasury in essence told the rest of the world that it was not only all right but almost desirable for them to let the value of the dollar fall in the foreign exchange markets. This policy even had an official name. It was called "benign neglect."

2. Every other nation was required to finance its external deficit by borrowing "real" money through the international banking system, i.e., money which that nation cannot itself create. But the U.S. was the world's banker. It could discharge the external obligations associated with its external deficits simply by giving creditors IOUs denominated in dollars. Our creditors could complain about this practice, and they did complain when the purchasing power of these IOUs began to fall, but they could do little else about the situation because our response was, "If you don't want these dollars, you can stop taking them; all you have to do is stop selling us your goods."

3. If any other nation had tried to behave this way, the rest of the world's response would have been quite predictable. Other countries would have stopped shipping their goods to such a nation. For most nations, such a threat of a cutoff in their imports would have meant disaster. But for the United States, the situation appeared to be wholly different. We are a large and continental economy. Except for oil, we can produce reasonable substitutes for most things we import. We are also the world's largest and most lucrative market. It is almost unthinkable that Japan would say to us, "You pay in real money, or no more Toyotas," or that the European Common Market countries would say to us, "Pay in real money or no more steel." About the only impact such reprisals would have in the United States is that the mayors of Detroit and Pittsburgh would each declare a three-day holiday of rejoicing and merriment!

Although the laws of economics grind slowly, they do grind. As the administration moved the U.S. economy on to an extremely fast growth track in 1977 and 1978, the U.S. did suffer a sharp increase in its balance-of-trade deficits. Because a nation's propensity to import is linked closely to its own internal growth rate, we sucked in imports, both of oil and nonoil commodities, at an increasing rate. By early 1978, the U.S. trade deficit had risen to the horrendous rate of $45 billion a year. To put this in perspective, *all* the trade deficits of *all* the deficit countries in the world in 1972 amounted to $10 billion a year.

The rest of the world tolerated our behavior for two reasons: First, there was not much they could do about it. Second, the behavior of the

U.S. was not entirely callous. Our choice of an expansive policy was driven not just by domestic political priorities regarding employment, but also by the plausibly noble idea that we could lead the world out of economic stagnation and high unemployment. The theory, put forth at a meeting of Western heads of state in 1977, was that if the United States would simply take the lead and if the two next largest economies in the world, Japan and West Germany, would follow our lead toward expansive economic policies, these three "locomotive" economies could pull the world onto a track of fast growth without any one nation suffering balance-of-payments consequences. There was some validity to this theory, which was in fact known for a while as the "locomotive theory." But the leaders of West Germany made it perfectly clear that they thought it would be an unwise, indeed foolish, policy to follow until inflation itself had been durably eradicated from the system. In retrospect they were right. Inflation had not been cured; it was simply quiescent, and it was soon to erupt again.

U.S. Policies Shift Slowly, But They Shift

It gradually began to dawn on U.S. policymakers that the policies they were pursuing had costs as well as benefits—and, worse still, that the costs were rising faster than the benefits. The sharp fall in the exchange rate of the dollar in 1977 and 1978 led to an equally sharp increase in the price we paid for our nonoil imports. Between early 1977 and the end of 1978, the exchange value of the German deutsche mark rose by over 30 percent against the U.S. dollar and the value of the Japanese yen by 45 percent. As the dollar's exchange value fell, the price of Japanese and German cars, for example, moved upward equally quickly. This in itself would not have added greatly to our domestic inflation rate because, of all the advanced countries in the world, we import the smallest fraction of the goods and services we consume. But there were significant second-round effects. In the context of rapidly rising prices for imports, our domestic manufacturers and the unions that bargain with them were able to raise their own prices and wages more rapidly than they otherwise might have done. By the end of 1978, average prices in the United States were rising more rapidly than in any other major industrial nation with the exception of Italy.

There was a second problem. The rest of the world holds a large volume of dollar assets of a highly liquid nature—bank accounts, Treasury bills, and Eurodollars (dollars on deposit outside the U.S.). As the purchasing power of the dollar fell, the threat increased that rational holders would begin to dump their dollars in the marketplace in exchange for anything else that promised to do a better job of maintaining its value. Had this dollar dumping been triggered, a crisis of large proportions would have occurred.

The third, and potentially the largest, threat came from the oil-producing states of the Arabian peninsula—an area in which a population of less than ten million people controls 50 percent of the free world's known reserves of petroleum and supplies 50 percent of the free world's oil imports.

In 1978 these countries began to feel increasingly disenchanted on two fronts:

1. The price of oil (which was denominated in U.S. dollars at around $12 per barrel) was falling rapidly in terms of the other currencies in which these Arab states purchased most of their imports. For example, between December 1973, when the new high price for oil was set, and October 1978 the value of the U.S. dollar fell by 50 percent against the Swiss franc—thanks to our 1977–78 policies of "benign neglect" with regard to both inflation and exchange rates. Rumblings that our policy was one of "malevolent neglect" began to surface.

2. Given their tiny populations, these countries were unable to spend all of their vast revenues and had therefore accumulated paper assets, mainly in U.S. dollars. Each time the U.S. economy misbehaved, the results eroded the value of their assets. By mid-1978 the erosion was becoming severe and painful.

As a result of these disenchantments, these Arab states began to ask three ominous questions:

1. "Why should we keep producing oil at close to our capacity limits? We do not need the money and leaving the oil in the ground is a far better investment than holding paper assets that keep falling in value." Had they acted accordingly the world would have been hit again by a serious shortage of oil similar to that of 1974.

2. "Why should we denominate our oil in U.S. dollars? If we had fixed the $12 price of 1974 in Swiss francs, the dollar price by late 1978 would have been $24 a barrel." Had the price of oil been denominated in some other, stronger currency, or a market basket of other currencies, this would have forced the U.S. to behave itself by adopting not only a sensible energy policy, but a sensible anti-inflationary policy, and a sensible exchange-rate policy as well.

3. "Why should we hold the bulk of our wealth in dollar-denominated securities that only fall in price and fall even faster in terms of purchasing power? Had this wealth been held in yen or deutsche mark or Swiss franc assets we would be twice as rich."

The three questions and their latent answers could not be safely ignored, especially not in light of the extremely negative political reactions of the Arab world to President Carter's preoccupation with Camp David talks between Egypt and Israel. In short, a group of oil-producing countries emerged in 1978 that could have said and might have said to the U.S., "Behave yourself, pay in real money, i.e., money you do not print yourself, or no more oil." Had they done so there would have been neither rejoicing nor merriment in the United States.

As the dollar began to fall very rapidly against other major currencies in September 1978, the reality of the situation dawned on the Carter administration. On Halloween Day, 1978, part of U.S. economic policy was put into a sharp U-turn. There were three basic components to the policy change:

1. With the full support of the president, the Federal Reserve System undertook to tighten our previously inflationary monetary policy. The signal for this change in policy was an increase in bank reserve requirements (i.e., the fraction of deposits banks are required to hold at the central bank) and a record one percentage point increase in the central bank's discount rate. By contrast, during the preceding two years, each attempt by the Federal Reserve to apply the monetary brakes with even so much as a one-quarter percent increase in the discount rate had been met by tongue lashings from monetary heavyweights on the White House staff.

2. We undertook to borrow "real" money, such as deutsche marks and Swiss francs, in order to finance part of our balance-of-payments deficits.

3. We gave up our previous policy of benign neglect and undertook to use the funds we borrowed in order to defend the value of the dollar at home and overseas.

What happened that Halloween was that we told the world we were at last prepared to give a far higher priority to such objectives as price stability, exchange-rate stability, and the reduction of our huge and rising dependence on imported oil—priorities that most of the rest of the world had adopted four years earlier. With these U.S. moves, the serious adaptation of the entire industrial world to the realities of the post-1973 era began.

The Second Oil Crisis, 1979–80

In 1979–80 the industrial world was struck by a second crisis, which was similar in some ways to what had struck it six years earlier, in 1973–74. Oil supplies were cut off, the price of oil took a huge jump, inflation worsened rapidly, and expansion gave way to recession. The events began in Iran.

Prior to the last quarter of 1978, Iran had been the second-largest oil

producer in OPEC and the second-largest exporter of oil. Iran produced nearly 6 million barrels per day (mb/d), about one-fifth of OPEC's total output, and exported 5½ million barrels per day of this to the free world. After the chaos that accompanied the overthrow of the Shah and the accession of the Ayatollah, Iran's oil output was cut by more than half in 1979 and exports dropped even more sharply. By early 1980, Iran's exports to the free world were down almost to zero. In just over a year, the supply of oil from Iran dropped by nearly 5 million barrels per day or by *more than the combined gross oil output of the North Sea, the Alaskan North Slope, and Mexico.* Long lines at gasoline stations appeared again, the price of oil traded in spot markets leaped as buyers scrambled to obtain supplies, and the basic price of oil rose by another quantum—from around $12 per barrel in October 1978 to $32 per barrel by mid-1980. On top of this very high base price, the more hawkish producers, such as Libya and Algeria, added large (and varying) "premiums" of $5 to $10 per barrel.

The 1979–80 jump in oil prices from $12 to $32 per barrel was smaller in percentage terms than the 1973–74 jump from $2 to $12; but it was twice as large in absolute terms. The sudden increase of $20 per barrel implied a staggering $200 billion increase in the world's already high annual bill for oil imports from OPEC. Because OPEC oil in 1979 accounted for nearly 50 percent of the free world's consumption of oil and natural gas, and because the price of the other 50 percent was also driven up by the OPEC price increase, the free world's total bill for all oil and gas rose by nearly $450 billion a year.

A useful way to think about what happened in 1979–80 is to view the oil price increase as the imposition of a tax on consumption of $450 billion a year—a massive tax increase by any standard. The results were predictable. The first impact of any large consumption tax is to accelerate the rate of inflation; the second is to trigger a recession. Both occurred in 1980.

The U.S. inflation rate, measured by our Consumer Price Index, which was already climbing rapidly in 1978 and 1979, jumped to 18 percent per annum in the first quarter of 1980. Other countries recorded even higher rates in early 1980, notably the U.K. (25 percent) and Italy (20 percent). Even in the best-behaved economies, such as West Germany and Japan, inflation accelerated.

Led by the U.S. and the U.K., the industrial world—with the sole exception of Japan—moved into a second post-OPEC recession in 1980–81. Thus the decade began with what looked like an inauspicious replay of what had occurred in 1974. But underneath the apparent similarity between the course of events after the first inflationary oil shock of 1973–74 and that after the second inflationary oil shock of 1979–80, there was a large and important difference: namely, the significant change that had taken place in the logic and thrust of the policy response to the three major problems that confronted the nation—inflation, energy, and the scope and role of government itself.

The Post-1974 Response

The response of U.S. policy after the shocks of 1973–74 is most aptly described by that old cliché, "business as usual," meaning, in this case, politics as usual.

Throughout 1977 and most of 1978 we continued to pursue highly expansionary fiscal and monetary policies with little regard to their inevitably inflationary consequences. We pushed our mindless quest for a lower unemployment rate through legislatively created and federally subsidized public-service jobs even though private employment was rising more rapidly than anybody had dreamed possible in the 1960s. We kept on suppressing interest rates payable to savers even though inflation and taxes had already made them negative. We kept on suppressing the price of oil and natural gas at levels far below the price we had to pay foreigners for equivalent forms of energy—a policy that vastly increased our reliance on Middle Eastern oil because it encouraged consumption and discouraged domestic production. We kept on increasing the pace at which the government spent, taxed, and intervened in the private sector.

The Post-1980 Response: Steps in the Right Direction

By the end of 1978 our policies began to shift, belatedly and grudgingly, but nonetheless decisively. We finally decided that the important objective of monetary policy was not to inflate the money supply in order to keep interest rates low and finance the government's deficits, but rather to prevent inflation. In intellectual terms this hardly ranks as a great discovery. In political terms it was a milestone.

We decided that our habit of suppressing the price of domestic oil and gas could have only one effect—to increase our vulnerable dependence on high-priced imported oil. We introduced the idea that oil and gas prices should be deregulated, albeit very, very gradually—intellectually a belated and miserable compromise but politically another significant step in the right direction.

These small and belated hacks at the dragons of inflation and energy mustered our courage to consider a hack at the largest dragon of all—a government that had lost control over itself. By early 1981 this idea too had become a reality. The Congress of the United States, prodded by a new president, was actually giving serious thought to the idea that cutting federal spending and federal taxes by about $40 billion might be the right medicine for what ailed the U.S. economy. Amazingly, by midyear a substantial cut in nondefense spending and in marginal tax rates had been enacted.

Is the shift in policy a countercurrent against a prevailing 15-year tide—or is it the beginning of a new tide? Only time will tell, but geography provides a clue. We map geographic watersheds not just by watching the direction in which the streams appear to flow but by the rivers into which they ultimately drain. Likewise, we map economic watersheds not just by the way in which the major economic variables seem to be moving, but by the way in which ideas and policies shift. By almost any reading of past history, the apparent movement of interest rates or of prices in general or of specific items such as gold or oil which we observed in the 1970s is not a reliable indicator of how those variables will move in the decade of the 1980s. A better indicator of the future might be the way in which ideas have shifted recently. But just where we go in the 1980s will depend on how tractable the problems of inflation, energy, and government prove to be now that the U.S. has decided that something must be done.

3

Inflation

INFLATION IS NOT ONLY THE MOST SERIOUS SYMPTOM of our contemporary economic problems, it is the principal cause of continuing illness in the economy. The erosion in the value of the dollar since the current tide of inflation began to rise in 1966 constitutes the gravest threat to our economic and political system since the persistent wave of unemployment that struck us in the 1930s. The chart on page 49 traces the mounting waves of inflation we have suffered over the past two decades. The inflation rate at each successive crest has been higher than that at the one preceding, and thus far the same has been true for the rate at each trough. The story is still incomplete. Whether the inflation rate at the next trough will fall below the 4.8 percent-a-year rate recorded at the end of 1976 we do not yet know. Nor do we know whether the 14.8 percent rate of inflation recorded between March 1979 and March 1980 represents the crest of crests, or whether it is simply another way station to still higher rates yet to come.

Theories of Inflation

After thinking about inflation for some 300 years, economists still do not have an agreed-upon theory of what causes chronic inflation or of how it can or should be halted. One reason for the lack of a true consensus is that economists are a cantankerous lot who defy labeling but love to attract labels. Their greatest joy, even beyond the cash and fame of Nobel prizes, is to have their names forever attached to a theory, or better still, a school of thought. One of their larger and more important disputes concerns the relation between money and inflation, i.e., the precise role that an increase in the quantity of money plays in determining the general level of prices.

The Monetarist School

At one extreme of contemporary economic opinion lie the true monetarists. To them, an increase in the quantity of money at a rate faster than the growth rate of real economic output is a *necessary* and *sufficient* condition for inflation: It is not only essential to any explanation of the phenomenon we can call inflation, but is, in itself, a completely sufficient explanation. Nothing else matters very much. Excessive monetary creation leads to excessive demand for goods and services and this phenomenon drives prices upward. If we stop excessive monetary creation, excess demand will abate and prices will stop rising.

The monetarist tradition goes back to at least a century before Adam Smith and probably even earlier. Its modern leader is unquestionably economist Milton Friedman. In his words, "Inflation is always and everywhere a monetary phenomenon."

In one sense, the monetarist school *must* be right. Prices (or the price level) represent the rate of exchange between money and commodities; hence any general rise in prices must involve money. The important question is whether general price inflation involves anything else.

The Cost-Push School

At the opposite extreme from the monetarist view we find the economists who believe that growth in the money supply is at most a passive and "enabling" partner in the process of modern inflation in developed industrialized countries such as the United States. To them, the true driving force behind general price increases is the upward push of costs—notably of wages, but also of such items as interest rates and energy costs. Many writers refer to this form of inflation, in which costs push prices up, as the "new inflation." In fact, the theory of cost-push inflation, as it is called, is almost as old as the monetary theory of inflation itself. The idea that the theory is relatively new stems from the fact that it has been restated in modern terms.

The current version of the theory is as follows. Today, labor unions have the power to raise the wages and fringe benefits their members enjoy at a rate faster than their productivity rises. This raises the labor cost of producing each unit of output. Since labor costs represent a huge

PERCENTAGE CHANGE IN
U.S. CONSUMER PRICE INDEX
(12-MONTH SPANS)

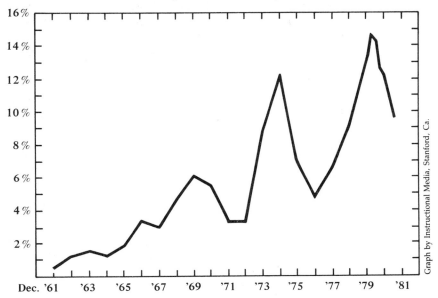

Graph by Instructional Media, Stanford, Ca.

fraction of total costs for most corporations, there is no way employers can finance such wage increases unless they in turn raise the prices of the products they sell. The fact that a few large corporations dominate many major industries gives these corporations the power to increase prices even under conditions where there is obviously no "excessive" demand for those products.

Recent history is rich with episodes of such behavior. For example, in the final months of 1980 the level of employment (the demand for labor) was lower than it had been in the final months of 1979. Because the labor force (the supply of labor) had been increasing, the unemployment rate (the excess supply of labor) rose from just under 6 percent at the end of 1979 to just under 7½ percent at the end of 1980. Many of the highly unionized industries—e.g., construction, autos, and steel—were suffering from very low levels of demand for their products relative to capacity. Nonetheless, between the end of 1979 and the end of 1980, compensation per hour of work *rose* at a rate of 10 percent. The cost-push school has a point: It is not easy to attribute this 10 percent rise to excessive demand!

Let us turn to the price side of the cost-push (or wage-push) view of events. In 1980, the universe of nonfinancial corporations paid a total labor-compensation bill that amounted to $1,037 billion for their domestic U.S. operations. According to official statistics, their aftertax profits from these activities were estimated at $60 billion for the year (out of which they paid cash dividends of $40 billion). An average 10 percent increase in their total wage costs amounts to some $104 billion a year. In the face of a falling volume of sales, there is obviously only one way in which these corporations can finance such an increase in their wage costs—that is to raise their selling prices. This is exactly what they did in 1980, and, according to cost-push theory, must always do if they do not wish to go bankrupt. A dramatic example of just such behavior was reported on the front page of the *Wall Street Journal* on April 6, 1981: "GM will raise new car prices 3.5% or $351 a unit. The boost, which raises its average sticker price to more than $10,200, surprised analysts and irritated some dealers. U.S. new car sales fell 17% in late March to 191,447 units as rebates were scaled back. The adjusted annual sales of 5.1 million units matches the level at the depths of the recession last May."

To put a rate of automobile sales of 5.1 million units per year in the U.S. in perspective, in 1973 the annual pace of sales of domestically produced cars was 9.7 million units. General Motors did not raise its prices in April 1981 because of excessive demand for its products; it raised prices because its costs were rising—thus goes the cost-push theory.

The essence of the cost-push argument is that once inflation accelerates—whether because of excessive monetary growth or because of external shocks such as a big leap in the price of petroleum—it will continue at its new level because large segments of labor will demand and get wage increases at close to the experienced rate of inflation. Unless offset by an increase in productivity, wage increases in turn will trigger price increases at around that rate. In short, wages chase prices upward, and in the next round of events prices chase wages. Once inflation has started, society as a whole is left with both wage increases and price increases chasing each other in orbit at some rate significantly above zero. The cost-push theorists refer to this rate of self-perpetuating inflation in a variety of ways—"built-in" inflation, "baseline" inflation, "embedded" inflation, "core" inflation, to name a few—all of which mean the same thing: There is a lot of inertia in modern price-wage movements; once they begin their joint upward move at some rate, they will tend to keep on going upward at that rate for a long time. What is more, as inflation itself persists, institutional arrangements evolve that serve to tighten the link between the two arms of the wage-price spiral.

Because the inflation we experienced in the 1970s brought with it a strengthening of the linkage between costs and prices, the current version of the cost-push theory of inflation is not as dependent as it used to be on the potential monopoly power of some unions and some corporations. It has become almost generalized into a broader "societal" view of why inflation persists in modern economies. Three principal developments have contributed to the emergence of the view that modern cost-push inflation has become a social phenomenon:

1. As inflation itself accelerated, labor, in making its periodic wage bargains, sought to lock in an increase in wages not only sufficient to offset past increases in prices but also flexible enough to offset future price increases. The obvious way to do this is through cost-of-living adjustments, referred to as COLAs by labor economists and as indexing by others. In 1970 only a few of the unions covered by large collective bargaining agreements were protected by cost-of-living clauses; today almost all of them demand such coverage. The existence of these formal escalator clauses increases the speed with which inflation spreads through the economy, and it also serves to perpetuate and thus "embed" into the system whatever inflation rate was last experienced.

2. Although the less-unionized sectors of society have not bargained as actively for indexation against price increases as have the large unions, the reality of full or partial indexation has nonetheless spread rapidly throughout the U.S. economy. Large flows of income such as Social Security benefits, federal government salaries, federal government retirement benefits, and welfare payments all have become substantially, fully, or sometimes more-than-fully and automatically indexed to an increase in the price level. For example, in early 1977 the legal minimum wage (the wage offered the least-powerful segment in society) was increased by congressional mandate from $2.30 an hour to $3.35 an hour by January 1, 1981—an increase of 46 percent in just over 36 months, a rate of increase actually greater than the rate of inflation for that period. In addition, Congress tied the rate of wages payable to another less-powerful segment in society—employees holding public-service employment jobs under our many "job creation" programs—at some fraction *above* the rising minimum wage. The total flow of income affected by such congressionally mandated indexation is no longer just a trivial portion of total income; indeed it far exceeds that earned by all workers in the entire manufacturing sector of the United States economy!

3. Finally, a decade of severe inflationary experience has created an embedded expectation of more inflation in the future. Consequently,

interest rates, another large element of cost in the total system, have also become yoked to whatever rate of inflation was last experienced. The same is true of taxes, another important cost element.

External Shocks

The cost-price interaction just discussed provides a useful insight to one modern phenomenon: Once inflation begins there are strong forces that keep it going. But this interaction does not in itself provide any answer as to why the rate of inflation has been *increasing*. In order to answer this question, the modern cost-push theorist looks to "external" shocks, i.e., large jumps in the price of items such as energy or food, neither of which is directly linked to the internal dance between domestic wages and domestic prices. We experienced several such shocks in the 1970s. From year-end 1972 to year-end 1973 food prices jumped 23 percent in 12 months, driven by much larger jumps in the prices of many agricultural products. A year later petroleum prices charged by oil exporters nearly quintupled. In 1979–80 they almost tripled again in another large jump. Each such price shock filters through the economy and in the process raises the general inflation rate. Then the cost-price interaction takes over to cement or embed the now higher rate of inflation into the system.

The Monetarist Counterattack

Economists who hold to the monetarist view of inflation—that a general increase in the price level is always and everywhere a monetary phenomenon—have not been noted for their tolerance of people, lay or professional, who argue that inflation is caused by a rise in costs. They are as intolerant of the cost-push argument and as unswayed by it in 1980 as they were back in 1800 when the battle between the two views first began.

Nearly 200 years ago when Britain suspended the gold standard during the long Napoleonic Wars, the prices of gold, silver, wheat, and most other commodities rose extremely rapidly. The then "cost-push" school argued that the major reasons for that large round of inflation were domestic crop failures, a disruption of trade (which led to price rises in particular commodities), and other such specific events whose effects eventually spread into a rise in the general price level. As is true of most of today's cost-push arguments, excessive monetary creation was not mentioned as a possible cause of that large rise in prices.

In early 1981 President Carter presented his final Economic Report to the nation. When, halfway through the report, the authors of his report finally got to the subject of inflation, they explained as follows: "The second inflationary surge which came in the early 1970s was associated with the first massive oil-price increase, a worldwide crop shortage which drove up food prices, and an economy which again became somewhat overheated in 1972 and 1973. The third inflationary episode came in 1979 and 1980. It was principally triggered by another massive oil-price increase, but part of the rise in inflation may also have been due to overall demand in the economy pressing on available supply" (*Economic Report of the President*, January 1981, pp. 7–8). As was true 180 years earlier, excessive monetary creation is not even mentioned, let alone stressed.

Back in the early 1800s the monetarist group (then known as Bullionists) blamed the rapid pace of price increases squarely on unrestrained monetary expansion by the Bank of England. The monetarists were then right. After the Napoleonic Wars, England went back to the gold standard, and this absolutely limited the power of the government to create money. Inflation stopped: In fact the price level *fell* for 30 years.

In 1844 the Bank of England became the United Kingdom's central bank, with the power to issue bank notes not backed by gold. Prices then began to rise and the argument over what drives inflation started all over again. Monetarists (then known as the Currency school of thought) were again pitted against the cost-pushers (then known as the Banking school). Once again the monetarists won. After the money supply was again brought under control, the price level, which had risen steadily from 1850 to 1870, began to fall and kept falling for 20 years.

The modern argument is not appreciably different from the debate that took place a century ago. Cost-pushers continue to blame inflation on crop failures, oil shocks, and such random events as the disappearance of anchovies off the coast of Peru in 1972. Monetarists continue to insist that the root cause of inflation and the real reason for its continuation is an excessive creation of money.

But there is a new and critical factor at play in the 1980s. This is the power that labor (unionized, nonunionized, or subsidized) now has to resist any decline in its money wages and its power to force employers (governmental or private) to raise wages approximately as fast as prices are rising. It is this issue that underlies the 1980s version of the old monetarist versus cost-push debate.

Implications for Policy

The dispute between modern monetarists and modern nonmonetarists is not just a continuation of an academic quarrel. It has enormous consequences for the conduct of national policy in the 1980s. The dichotomy is dramatic, as is pointed up by the following:

If the monetarists are right, the inflation we are now suffering can be cured by reining in the rate at which the government creates money. Furthermore, such a cure for our most pressing economic disease can be accomplished within the context of a system of free markets and individual choice.

If, on the other hand, the cost-push school is right in the context of conditions in the 1980s, modern inflation cannot be corrected within a system of free markets. At the minimum, the rate at which wages and other income payments are allowed to increase will have to be restrained by government edict until those increases abate to a rate *no greater* than the nation's average rate of increase in productivity.

The Convergence of Theory

The sharpness of the split in views posited above is literally accurate only for the two extremities of contemporary opinion. A large group in the middle is prepared to accept a melding of the two theories, as far as *theory* goes. But even for them, a sharp split on *policy* prescriptions remains.

So far as theory is concerned, most modern cost-pushers now concede that money very frequently has a great deal to do with how inflation begins in the first place. They also concede that expectations about how monetary policy will be conducted in the future are an important ingredient in the link between experienced inflation and future inflationary pressures. Finally they concede that a continuing increase in the supply of money is necessary in order to ratify and thus embed an ongoing rate of inflation.

Likewise, most monetarists are now willing to concede that the widespread presence of cost-push factors and frequent occurrences of external shocks are huge barriers to disinflating (reducing the rate of inflation) via more stringent control over the pace of monetary growth.

The new disagreement therefore centers around the question of whether monetary control can or cannot tame inflation in the early 1980s without wrecking economic growth or even the society we seek to preserve. The modern monetarists think that it can be done; the modern cost-pushers believe that it cannot. Although it is couched in different terms, the new split is as irreconcilable as its more theoretical ancestor was 10, 25, or 200 years ago. Indeed, in some ways the paradox of an apparent convergence of theory without any real agreement on the policy front worsens the task any expositor faces. We must now address two issues: What caused the acceleration in our inflation from under

1½ percent before 1965 to 15 percent in early 1980? And, given modern complications, what is the least costly way of getting that rate back down to 1½ percent a year?

Policy Triggers Inflationary Spiral, 1965–70

Today there is little dissent from the general belief that ill-conceived U.S. policy was initially responsible for kicking off the wave of accelerating price increases that started in 1966. That triggering was not caused by President Johnson's 1965 decision to wage a limited war in Vietnam and an unlimited war on poverty at home. The real cause was his insistence on a policy of "Guns, Butter, *and* the Great Society"—all with no increase in taxes to offset the inevitable increase in total spending which that package of policies ensured.

The evidence on inflation for the free world's seven largest economies and Switzerland is summarized in Table 2. The first column of the table shows clearly that up to 1965 the U.S. had been the best-behaved large economy with regard to price inflation. Excluding Canada, which is closely tied to the U.S. because 70 percent of her trade is with us, the average annual rate of inflation in the six significant industrial economies outside the U.S. was over *triple* our rate—3.7 percent a year for them as contrasted with 1.2 percent for the U.S.

After 1965 the U.S. rate of inflation accelerated rapidly. By 1969 it was running at over 6 percent a year—the highest rate of inflation of the eight major economies covered in Table 2. The quintupling of the U.S. inflation rate between the pre-1965 years and 1969 was a straightforward monetary phenomenon—the kind documented in almost every introductory economics textbook and demonstrated frequently in countries such as Argentina and Brazil.

The Vietnam War

The Vietnam War increased U.S. defense spending from $50 billion a year in 1965 to $80 billion by the end of 1968—an increase of over 50 percent. Given the sleight of hand that is frequently practiced in federal budgeting, the actual increase was probably even greater. Defense spending adds to the purchasing power of all those who receive the monies spent, but it adds nothing in the way of tangible goods and services that people can buy. The obvious and inevitable result, when the recipients of the added defense dollars spend all or part of their receipts, is an upward pressure on prices.

Great Society Programs

The contemporaneous increase in spending for President Johnson's

Table 2: Average Annual Change in Consumer Prices, Selected Periods
(percent per annum)*

	Pre-Vietnam 1959–65	Vietnam 1968–69	Nixon 1971–72	1st Oil Crisis 1973–74	Ford 1975–76	Carter 1977–78	2nd Oil Crisis 1978–79	1980–81**
U.S.	1.2	6.1	3.3	12.2	4.8	9.0	13.3	9.8
Canada	1.5	4.6	4.8	12.0	5.9	8.8	9.8	12.6
Other Countries								
Japan	5.6	6.0	4.5	24.4	9.4	3.5	5.8	5.2
West Germany	2.6	2.9	5.6	6.4	3.8	2.4	5.4	5.6
France	3.8	5.7	5.8	15.0	9.9	9.5	11.8	12.8
United Kingdom	2.9	5.1	7.2	18.4	14.0	8.0	17.2	11.7
Italy	4.5	4.0	5.8	25.8	21.0	11.5	19.8	20.4
Switzerland	2.9	2.3	6.9	8.7	1.0	0.6	5.2	6.3
Unweighted average (6 other countries)	3.7	4.3	6.0	16.5	9.9	5.9	10.9	10.3

*From end of initial year indicated to end of terminal year indicated. U.S. data from December to December.
**From second quarter 1980 to second quarter 1981.

Sources: U.S. data from *Economic Report of the President, 1979*. Data for other countries from the Federal Reserve Board, St. Louis, *International Economic Conditions*, quarterly issues.

Great Society programs had the same kind of inflationary effect. The big difference is that the expenditures for these programs have kept on rising, and, unless they are curbed drastically, they will probably keep on rising for decades. By definition, welfare spending puts spendable funds in the hands of people who do not contribute any significant increase to the supply side of the economic equation. Between 1965 and 1973, transfer payments by the U.S. government to society (a proxy for welfare-related spending) *tripled* from around $40 billion a year to $120 billion, including a tenfold increase in federal expenditures on health care programs and a sixfold increase in education and manpower programs.

The rise in *private* spending power brought about by a rise in federal defense and welfare spending *need not* lead to price inflation in the society in which it occurs. A corresponding increase in taxes, which withdraws an equal amount of spending power from the economy, would balance the federal budget and thus neutralize the equation—at least in the short run. But tax increases are almost always unpopular, and all who dwell in Washington have a passionate distaste for unpopularity. So taxes were not raised until mounting evidence of serious inflation forced the government to act in late 1968, more than three years later than it should have acted. By then the damage had been done.

The interesting question is whether anybody in the Johnson administration even thought about such an honest solution to the problem as a tax increase. We do not know, because, with regard to economic policy, 1965 is one of the least-documented years in recent U.S. history. The best guess is that one or more advisers suggested in 1965 that a tax increase might be the correct way to ward off inflation—and that the president removed them bodily from the Oval Office.

The Role of the Federal Reserve

The U.S. has a second line of defense against inflation—the Federal Reserve System (referred to as the Fed), whose principal purpose is to control society's supply of money. In one sense the tools at its disposal are as powerful as those wielded by the president and the Congress through the federal budget. For example, even the unwise policy decisions of the administration in 1965 and following years—to increase defense and welfare spending without an increase in taxes—need not have led to the price inflation we suffered. Had it chosen to do so, the Fed could have refused to accommodate the government's potentially inflationary policies. It could have done this by not buying any of the new debt the government was issuing. The federal government would have been forced to go to the private credit market to raise the growing

Drawing by MacNelly
© 1979 MacNelly in *The Richmond News Leader*

difference between what the government took in in taxes and the even larger amounts it wanted to spend. Given the ability of the federal government to command credit, the private sectors—business, housing, and consumers—would have been denied part of the flow of credit on which they regularly depend. Interest rates would have been driven to very high levels, but private spending would have been curbed and the rate of inflation would have been held close to its pre-1965 level.

But the Fed did not choose to exercise this option. It tried it briefly in 1966 and then backed off. Through most of the period from 1966 to 1969, it actively purchased enough of the federal government's new issue of debt (the counterpart of the government's deficit) to prevent the severe crimp in credit and the rise in interest rates that might have occurred. As a result, money was created too fast and inflation accelerated.

The Money-Creation Process

But how exactly is money created and what is the connection between budget deficits and money creation in modern societies?

We speak of the government "printing press" in connection with the process of modern money creation, but the process is far more subtle than merely printing more money and putting it in circulation. Most of what serves as modern money is not the printed currency notes we use, but transactions or demand deposits (held mainly at commercial banks, but also since 1981 at other financial institutions—mutual savings banks, savings and loan associations, and credit unions) that we can transfer to one another through checks. The check itself is not money; it is simply the mechanism for transferring money. Money is the checking deposit against which our checks can be written. It thus follows that any action that creates more checkable deposits in a society creates more money.

In the United States, as in most countries, the power to create new money—i.e., to increase the aggregate volume of checkable deposits in existence—is shared by two sets of institutions. One is the nation's central bank, in the U.S. the Federal Reserve System. The other is the commercial banking system taken as a whole. Most countries have a few large banks with nationwide branching powers. For some inexplicable reason the U.S. has over 14,000 banks, and since January 1981 nearly 40,000 "banking" institutions. (Effective January 1, 1981, mutual savings banks, savings and loan associations, and credit unions have been empowered to offer checkable accounts to the public. In this sense they have become banks.)

You and I and General Motors generally hold our checking deposits at commercial banks. Those banks in turn hold *their* checking deposits either at another commercial bank, or more importantly, at one of the 12 Federal Reserve banks that comprise the Federal Reserve System. They use these deposits to settle their debts or credits against one another. The deposits held at the Fed are also known as "reserves" because all institutions that are allowed to offer the public checking deposits are also required by law to hold a stipulated fraction (e.g., 10 percent) of *their* deposit liabilities to the public in the form of a non-interest-bearing deposit at the Fed. For large banks, these reserve requirements are calculated and met weekly—for smaller institutions, on a biweekly basis.

Banks that fail to meet these requirements are subject to penalties; however, the real pressure to meet reserve requirements is the huge adverse publicity any delinquent institution is likely to encounter. Some commercial banks have been willing to give up membership in the Federal Reserve System to escape the onerous burden of having to hold part of their assets in the form of non-interest-bearing reserves, but thus far no bank, while still a member, has ever failed to meet its stipulated reserve requirement.

So much for background. Now to the process of modern money creation. When you or I lend something to someone else, e.g., a car or a lawnmower, we temporarily give up the use of the asset we lend. The same is true when we lend money. That is not the case when a commercial bank lends. What a commercial bank does when it makes a loan is give the borrower a checkable deposit account which that borrower did not have before. In exchange, the bank gets an asset that did not exist before—namely the borrower's IOU or promissory note or bond. After the transaction, there is a larger volume of checkable deposits in society than existed before the bank loan was consummated. New money has been created. This money can be spent to buy goods and services just as readily as you or I can spend the paycheck we deposit in a bank.

The power of a bank, or of the banking system collectively, to create new deposits and hence new money is not unlimited. It is strictly limited by their need to hold reserves at the Fed equal to some stipulated fraction of their total deposit liabilities to the public. And thus we come to the true wellspring on which the entire process of modern money creation rests—the Federal Reserve System itself.

The total volume of reserve deposits that banks collectively hold at the Fed at any point in time is fixed. It will remain fixed until the Fed itself chooses to change it. One bank can obtain an extra dollar of reserves over and above what it had been holding, but only at the expense of some other bank losing a dollar of its reserves. For example, assume that I pay you $100 by giving you a check drawn on my account at Wells Fargo, and that you deposit this check to your account at Bank of America. Assume for simplicity that no other transactions take place in society that day. Wells Fargo will somehow have to pay the Bank of America $100. It does so through its account at the Fed, which simply transfers $100 from Wells Fargo's reserve account to the Bank of America's reserve account. The total volume of reserves collectively held by Wells Fargo and the Bank of America is unchanged. So is the total volume of reserves collectively held by all banks. So therefore is the total volume of deposits held by the public. Neither the volume of reserves nor the volume of deposits to which reserves are linked can increase until the Fed decides to create new reserves.

The Source of New Reserves

How then *does* the Fed create new reserves for the banks to hold so that the banks in turn can create new money by making more loans than were previously outstanding? The process is quite simple. The Fed creates new reserves whenever it acquires an asset. Obviously the Fed is not free to buy and record as an asset absolutely anything it chooses. Its freedom is limited by laws passed by Congress. It cannot, for example, buy Rembrandt paintings (or we would be on a Rembrandt standard) or wheat (or we would be on a wheat standard). The principal assets eligible for purchase by the Fed have been:

1. Gold or gold certificates (i.e., claims against gold owned by the U.S. Treasury). When a nation is on a pure gold standard, this is the *only* asset its central bank may acquire, and its stock of money can grow only as its stock of gold increases.

2. Government "paper," i.e., securities such as Treasury bills, notes, or bonds issued by the U.S. government, or government agency "paper," i.e., securities issued by major federal agencies (such as the Federal Home Loan Bank) and fully guaranteed by the U.S. government itself. Over the past 30 years government paper has been far and away the dominant type of asset acquired by the Fed. This is why we frequently refer to our present standard as a "paper" standard.

3. The freely convertible foreign currencies such as deutsche marks or Swiss francs. For the Fed, the actual purchase of such assets is a very recent phenomenon. By contrast, for most *other* central banks, the purchase of U.S. dollars (the premier convertible foreign currency) represents the principal form of asset acquisition since World War II. That is why some writers argue that the postwar world has been on a "dollar" standard.

Let us say the Fed decides to purchase $1 billion of Treasury securities. It does not have to give up, as you or I would, some other asset to accomplish this purchase. All it gives the seller of the securities is a check drawn on itself, i.e., its own liability for the $1 billion in the form of a deposit withdrawable from the Fed itself. The seller of the $1 billion of Treasury securities gets an asset that never existed before. What he gets is $1 billion of newly created money. Once the seller gets this newly created money, he cannot destroy it. All he can do is pass it on to someone else. Once created the new money stays in the system. Only the Fed can destroy what it has created—by the reverse process of selling Treasury securities from its portfolio.

U.S. Money Creation, 1965–70

The process described above completes the explanation of how President Johnson triggered the inflationary spiral that began in 1965. He decided that the U.S. government should increase expenditures without raising taxes. So the U.S. government had to borrow the difference. The new debt the president issued to accomplish this borrowing was *not* new money—it was simply U.S. government debt. Had it all been sold to the private sector, that increase in the government debt would *not* have led to rapid growth in the money supply, which in turn led to a serious acceleration in inflation; it would have led to one mad competition for loanable funds that would have driven interest rates to the sky. Credit for housing would have dried up; consumers, small businesses, and farmers would have had to scramble for funds to keep going; and the wrath of Congress would have descended on everybody except the real culprit, namely Congress itself. To prevent a serious credit crunch and the risk of recession such a crunch would have entailed, the Fed decided to buy a sizeable part of the new debt that President Johnson issued. From December 1965 to December 1970, the gross federal debt rose by $68 billion, or 21 percent, from $321 billion to $389 billion. Federal debt held by the Fed rose by over 50 percent from $41 billion to $62 billion. Other federal government accounts, such as the social insurance trust funds, bought $38 billion. The private sector bought only $9 billion of the $68 billion of new debt issued. When the U.S. government buys its own IOUs on a large scale, inflation can never be far behind.

Of course, one does not see all this happening on a day-to-day basis. Law and propriety do not permit the Fed to buy new issues of U.S. government securities directly from the Treasury except in the most extreme emergencies. The new securities are sold to the public. But the Fed can and did buy large amounts of previously issued government securities in the open market, thus creating the increased bank reserves and consequently the increased money supply that allowed the public to keep on spending at a rising rate. Propriety was maintained, but sin was nonetheless committed. More than a decade later society is still paying for those sins.

The Printing Press Goes Worldwide, 1971–73

Between 1965 and 1969 the U.S. government created the first of three very large imbalances in our system: It increased the stock of money and thus the pressure of demand for goods and services to a level far higher than the flow of available supply of goods and services could satisfy at existing prices. The price level in the U.S. rose to match the new and higher level of money supply and the enlarged demand for goods and services that such an augmented money supply fueled. What we suffering observers saw as an acceleration in the inflation rate was simply an upward adjustment of prices to a level commensurate with the preceding expansion in the supply of money.

But why did the adjustment process (the rise in U.S. prices) not come to a stop or slowdown in 1970 after that corrective jump had taken place? The answer is that it did. By 1971 the rate of inflation had fallen from over 6 percent a year in 1969 to under 3.5 percent. The inflation rate probably would have fallen even further if a new wave of world-wide inflation had not been set in motion in that year.

To understand what happened on a worldwide basis in 1971, 1972, and 1973, it is necessary to begin with the structure of the postwar international monetary system and the critical role that the U.S. dollar played in it.

The Bretton Woods System

Back in 1946, the trading world, tired of the prewar chaos that had prevailed in international exchange rates and wary of a return to those conditions, designed a system of stable exchange rates built around the U.S. dollar. The system—known as Bretton Woods, after the New Hampshire town in which the original agreements were signed—worked well for two decades. Between 1949, when they were actually put into full operation, and 1971, the dollar-linked set of exchange rates among the major trading nations remained remarkably stable. The exchange rate between Japan (the free world's second-largest economy) and the U.S. was a constant 360 yen to 1 dollar throughout the period. The exchange rate between West Germany (the free world's third-largest economy) and the U.S. was changed just once, in 1961, when the deutsche mark was revalued upward by 5 percent. The rate between the U.K. pound and the dollar was also changed only once: In 1967 the United Kingdom devalued the pound from $2.80 to $2.40. This gave American tourists in Britain a brief respite from having to do any currency translating because one British penny was for a time exactly equal to one American cent. That respite ended when Britain then decided to decimalize her coinage by introducing "new pence." France, the free world's fourth-largest economy, devalued twice, once in 1958 following the Algerian War and again in 1968 after student riots disrupted the French economy in the spring of that year. Throughout the period the exchange rate between the U.S. dollar and the Swiss franc was as fixed as the rate between a dollar in New York and a dollar in California!

The Role of the Dollar

One reason for the stability of the international monetary system prior to 1971 was the unusual role that the U.S. dollar played during the decades after Bretton Woods. The dollar served the world as international money. Nothing can serve in this unique role unless it possesses a critically balanced blend of two characteristics:

1. It must be desired. People and institutions must be willing to accept

and to hold it. The latter in turn depends on the former: The willingness to hold money issued by a foreigner rests on a general confidence that other people and institutions will always be willing to accept it.

2. It must be available. Something not available, no matter how desirable, obviously cannot serve as money. It is as simple as that. But if too much of it is available, the first characteristic will be lost.

The U.S. dollar prior to the late 1960s combined both characteristics in a proper blend. As an advanced and diversified producer, the U.S. offered the rest of the world an enormous variety of goods and services: raw materials (even petroleum before 1970!); food and fiber; high technology products; medical, educational, and training services; and a huge range of consumer products. As a result, the U.S. had run a chronic surplus in its balance of trade with the rest of the world, year after year, for over 75 years prior to 1971. One reason the rest of the world desired the dollar was the belief that they, or at least someone else, could always find use for the dollar to finance their collective trade deficit with the United States.

If international transactions had been confined to trade alone, there would have been a chronic shortage of dollars in the world outside the U.S.—i.e., the dollar, no matter how desirable, could not have served the world as an international medium of exchange and settlement because the pool of dollars available to the rest of the world would have been too small relative to the growing flow of international trade. But transactions between the U.S. and the rest of the world involve far more than trade. There are private remittances, government grants and loans, business investments, tourist and military expenditures, and a host of other transactions that generate inflows or outflows of dollars. On all these nontrade accounts, collectively, there was a large and steady net outflow of dollars. Because of these outflows, U.S. citizens by 1970 had accumulated some $170 billion of assets in the rest of the world, mainly in the form of corporate long-term investments. But over the same period, the rest of the world had accumulated some $100 billion of assets or claims against the U.S., of which some $50 billion was in the form of liquid or near-liquid dollars such as Treasury bills, certificates of deposit, and the like. This was the pool of dollars that served the world as international money.

Although there was a yearly *inflow* of dollars to the U.S. on its basic trading account (which made the dollar desirable), there was also a larger yearly *outflow* of dollars because of our other transactions (which made the dollar available). Thus did the dollar serve two potentially conflicting ordinances, desirability and availability, until it fell from grace in 1971.

The Erosion of Confidence

Under the pressures of demand induced when the Vietnam War was piled on top of the Great Society, two things happened. First, our demand for goods and services from the rest of the world rose more sharply than did their demand for our products. Second, our rate of inflation rose to exceed the rate of inflation of our major trading partners, which meant we were losing one important competitive edge. The two developments caused our basic trade balance to swing from a trade surplus to a deficit in 1971—our first trade deficit since 1893.

To some observers, the swing of the U.S. trade balance to deficit in 1971 was a temporary aberration: The deficit would disappear when the already subsiding pressure of the Vietnam War finally dissipated. If the deficit still remained, the situation could be corrected by pressing other nations, especially Japan, to give our products the same degree of access to their markets as we allowed theirs in ours.

Other, shrewder observers viewed the U.S. swing into a trading deficit in 1971 as the result of more fundamental forces. Whereas the U.S. had formerly been largely self-sufficient, America had now become hooked on foreign oil, foreign cars, and foreign steel. The nation that had once been the world's largest producer of all three of these commodities had been overtaken rapidly by foreign competition. Indeed, by the early 1970s, we had become the world's largest *importer* of all three. When it became evident that our trade deficit might be a truly chronic phenomenon, a major reason for the world to hold dollars disappeared.

To our steady deficit on nontrade transactions, there was now added in 1971 the new deficit on trade. As long as that trade deficit persisted, each year more dollars would be available to the world than the world needed in that year to buy our goods. On top of that, the rest of the world was holding around $50 billion in liquid dollar balances that they had voluntarily accumulated over the postwar decades, in part because those dollar balances might be needed to finance prospective deficits in their collective balance of trade with the U.S.

When the world's deficit with the U.S. turned into surplus in 1971 and our deficit emerged, only one possible motive was left for other countries to hold those liquid dollar assets. This was the investment motive: Rational people and governments will hold assets that offer the best possible combination of *safety, income* (in this case, interest income) and *appreciation* (in this case, a potential rise in the value of the dollar relative to alternative currencies). On all three counts, the U.S. dollar suffered large setbacks in 1971:

1. Prior to 1971 dollars held by foreign central banks were legally convertible into gold at the U.S. Treasury at the fixed rate of $35 to 1 troy ounce. On August 15, 1971, we closed the gold window; that is, we suspended convertibility of dollars into gold at a set price. For dollar holders abroad a certain amount of safety vanished.

2. From William Jennings Bryan to Jimmy Carter, populist tradition in America has sought to keep interest rates as low as possible. Throughout most of the postwar period, our interest rates were lower than rates in other economies: If West Germany and Switzerland are excluded, U.S. interest rates were much lower than rates that prevailed elsewhere. After rising in 1969–70, U.S. interest rates had fallen by 1971 to levels that were low by world standards. In 1971 and 1972 the income motive for holding dollars vanished.

3. The disappearance of both the safety motive for holding dollars and the income motive for holding dollars was important but small relative to the disappearance of the potential appreciation motive for holding dollars. From 1946 to 1971 the U.S. dollar had lost exchange value only once, and then by only 5 percent against one currency, the German deutsche mark, which had been deliberately undervalued from the postwar day on which it had come into existence. In all of the other 100 or more revaluations that occurred between 1946 and 1970, the dollar's value had appreciated every time. Although U.S. interest rates were low relative to interest rates offered in other currencies between 1946 and 1971, the exchange value of the dollar had been rising so that the total expected return to investors was generally better than they could have earned through investment in assets denominated in other currencies. In 1971 this plus factor was reversed as well.

Devaluing the Dollar

When the external supply of one country's currency is palpably in excess of the rest of the world's demand for it, huge pressures develop for a downward change in its "price," i.e., for a devaluation of that currency against other currencies. That is what happens to Brazil every month, what happened to France in 1958 and 1968, and to the U.K. in 1967.

The problem with the need to devalue the U.S. dollar in 1971 was that nobody quite knew how to go about it! The dollar-centered system on which the entire international exchange-rate mechanism had been based after 1946 had not foreseen that the dollar itself might someday have to be devalued against *all* other strong currencies.

Under the fixed, but alterable, exchange-rate system known as Bretton Woods, the U.S. dollar played a central role—but also a passive role.

"It's a novel about interest rates."

The dollar was pegged to gold at $35 per troy ounce. This peg was maintained by the willingness of the U.S. Treasury to buy gold from or sell gold to the central bank of any other member nation at $35 per ounce minus or plus some trivial fraction. Each of the other major nations pegged its currency to the U.S. dollar at a stated rate known as that currency's *par value*. And each central bank agreed to maintain the external value of its currency within a narrow band of plus or minus 1 percent around its par value, by using U.S. dollars to buy its currency (when its currency fell to 1 percent below its par value) or by using its own currency to buy and hold U.S. dollars (when the currency rose to 1 percent above its par value). Thus the par value for the Japanese yen was set at 360 yen to 1 dollar and that rate was maintained by the willingness (and ability) of the Bank of Japan to buy all foreign-held yen offered to it by paying dollars (1 dollar per 360 yen) and to buy all dollars offered to it by paying yen (360 yen per 1 dollar). Thus the yen/dollar exchange rate was entirely a Japanese responsibility and maintained in Tokyo. The same was true for all the other major exchange rates: The deutsche mark/dollar rate was maintained in Frankfurt, the French franc/dollar rate in Paris, the U.K. pound/dollar rate in London, and so on.

In order for any country other than the U.S. to devalue, all it had to do was announce a change in the rate at which its currency would be pegged to the dollar. For devaluations greater than 10 percent, international approval (i.e., the approval of the U.S., which had veto power) was required, but that rarely took long.

But how could the U.S. devalue the dollar when it needed to in 1971? Theoretically we could have changed the par value of the dollar by raising the price at which we were willing to buy and sell gold from $35 per ounce to something higher, for example, $50 per ounce. But this in itself would not have altered the dollar's exchange rate against the yen (the 360 to 1 rate was *entirely* up to Tokyo) or against any other currency.

The truth was that in 1971 we were the only nation that did not have the power to change the foreign exchange value of its currency. Playing the role of the world's central currency had a lot of advantages, but it also had some problems. The exchange value of the dollar against each major currency was one item that was not determined in Washington or New York; it was determined in Tokyo, Frankfurt, Paris, London, Rome, Toronto, Amsterdam, and all the other financial centers of the world.

The only way the dollar could be devalued was for each of those countries to revalue its currency upward against the dollar. Each of our major trading partners was quite unwilling to do anything of the kind unless all agreed to do likewise. Why? Let us take Japan as an example. In early 1971 the Japanese yen was pegged in Tokyo, as previously noted, at 360 yen to 1 dollar. At the same time the French franc was pegged in Paris at 5.56 francs to 1 dollar. Given these two pegs it follows that the cross-rate between the Japanese yen and the French franc must be very close to 360/5.56 yen to 1 franc or about 65 yen to 1 French franc.

Now to the point. Let us assume the government of Japan agrees that the dollar should be devalued by 20 percent, from 360 yen per dollar to 288 yen per dollar. However the French do not go along and continue to maintain the old franc/dollar rate of 5.56 francs per 1 dollar. Japan will find that against the franc the yen will rise from its old value of 65 yen per 1 franc to 51.8 yen per 1 franc. In brief, no single country could revalue its currency upward relative to the dollar without also doing so relative to every other currency, *unless everybody moved by the same percentage at the same time.*

The Resistance to Revaluation

With enough goodwill and intelligence, this could have been done. The dollar could have been devalued by all other nations revaluing their currencies upward in concert. In the real world this was asking too much: A dozen nations would have had to do something that was generous and sensible, and do so simultaneously. Understandably, they did not. Everybody wanted to revalue by *less* than everybody else—a major motive being that each country desired to maximize the competitiveness of its exports in the huge U.S. market and in other markets as well. Such upward revaluation would *decrease* their competitiveness in foreign markets.

For many continental countries, notably France, there were additional motives for their governments to resist revaluing upward against the dollar. With the French franc pegged at 5.56 francs to 1 dollar, and the dollar pegged to gold at $35 per ounce, it follows that the franc price of gold is 194.6 francs per ounce. Assume France agrees to revalue the franc upward against the dollar to a new rate of 4.63 francs to 1 dollar. If the dollar price of gold is left unchanged at $35 per ounce, then the franc price of gold will *fall* from its old value of 194.6 francs to 162.2 francs per ounce. But for generations, Frenchmen have been slipping gold Napoleons or kilogram bars of gold under the mattress, a rational Gallic behavior based on the historically undisputed experience that the price of gold against the franc has risen for centuries. It was also clear from his speeches on the subject that their leader in the late 1960s, General Charles de Gaulle, shared his countrymen's enthusiasm for the yellow metal. How then could his successor, Georges Pompidou, do something that would bring the franc price of gold down? Even more, how could he do a thing like that to help solve a problem that was not a French problem at all, but a purely American one? The answer is that he could not and would not. But if France, or any other major nation, would not agree to revalue its currency, nobody else would either, so the problem of dollar devaluation was back at square one.

To make matters even less tractable, each member of the European Common Market had an additional reason for believing that an upward revaluation of its currency would be unpopular with its politically powerful farmers. Common Market subsidies to agriculture were set in U.S. dollars. After any upward revaluation, a farmer whose subsidy was set in dollars would receive fewer francs or deutsche marks than before, and he would not look kindly on a government that subjected him to that kind of treatment!

The many obstacles abroad to a swift and decisive readjustment of the dollar against other currencies were compounded by two obstacles of our own creation:

1. The first obstacle was an unwillingness to believe that a devaluation of the U.S. dollar was the only feasible remedy for the serious imbalance in our international trade and payments position. In early 1971 many groups within the Nixon administration were of the opinion that the worsening imbalance in our trade in large part was caused by the unwillingness of Europe and Japan to allow our products the same free access to their markets as we allowed their products in our market. To these groups, the proper cure was not for us to devalue the dollar but for us to insist on a fairer set of tariff, tax, and trading arrangements.

2. The second obstacle arose out of U.S. views regarding the role of gold in the system. For example, there was one way in which the U.S. could have devalued the dollar to a new level *relative* to all other major currencies: It could have devalued relative to gold (i.e., increased the dollar price of gold) while at the same time demanding that other countries maintain the former parity of their currencies to gold. This route was not followed for a number of reasons.

Many believed that gold no longer had a role to play in a modern international exchange-rate system. The only exchange rates that mattered were those between the major currencies. The price of gold was neither relevant nor useful in this context. This group wanted once and for all to eliminate the vestigial role of gold from the international monetary system just as it had earlier been removed from our national monetary system.

Others believed that any system of fixed parities, with or without a gold link, was a form of artificial price fixing that simply perverted underlying market forces and thus prevented the attainment of a true equilibrium. They wanted to use the opportunity that presented itself in 1971 to switch to a system of floating exchange rates that would be determined freely in the marketplace.

Some were reluctant to raise the price of gold because the principal immediate beneficiaries of such an action would be the two major gold-producing countries, South Africa and the Soviet Union, plus those individuals and nations who had deliberately switched their wealth out of U.S. dollars into gold. None of these potential beneficiaries of an increase in the price of gold ranked high on the popularity list of those who are or see themselves as opinion makers.

In addition, there were legal and political obstacles. When the Congress ratified the Bretton Woods Agreement in 1945, it also eliminated the power of the executive branch to propose or agree to any change in the gold value of the dollar without prior congressional authority. In the context both of politics and events in early 1971, a request from the president to raise the dollar price of gold would have led to lengthy debates in Congress and also to an avalanche of speculative dollar outflows while Congress debated. Nor did the incumbent president relish the prospect of being dubbed by the media as the primary author of the dollar's devaluation and hence by inference the author of whatever mismanagement had led to the dollar's plight.

Market Pressures, 1971–73

As 1971 opened it was clear that U.S. transactions with its major trading partners were in a state of serious imbalance. To put it another way, at the then prevailing exchange rates between the dollar and other principal currencies, the total supply of dollars available in the world's principal foreign exchange markets was far larger than the demand for dollars in those markets. In a free market the "price" of the dollar (i.e., the exchange rate) would have rapidly fallen to its proper level, that is, the level at which the excess supply of dollars would be eliminated. But the market was not free. Exchange rates in each market were pegged at a preset level and maintained there by the willingness of each foreign central bank to mop up the excess supply of dollars entering the market by buying them at the preset price.

Recall that every time these central banks bought a dollar they *created* new money because they had to issue more of their own currencies to cover each purchase. Given its money-creating side effect, the policy of trying to maintain the dollar's price above its proper level was a potentially dangerous one. It was nonetheless pursued, with varying intensity, for two full years—from March 1971 to March 1973. In the process these misguided policies produced a very large increase in the world's money supply before they were finally abandoned in the second quarter of 1973 when most major nations allowed their currencies to float, more or less freely, against the dollar. By mid-1973 the exchange value of the dollar had fallen to levels dictated by the forces of demand and supply.

The Extent of Global Money Creation

We can measure the amount of international money creation in two ways. One way is to ask how much of its own money each major country created. The answer is that in Japan and the seven European nations that carry a large influence in world financial matters, the average expansion in the domestic money supply was a huge *45 percent* between year-end 1970 and mid-1973, a compound annual rate of nearly 16 percent a year! The inflation that followed in all of these countries during 1973 and 1974 was obviously fueled by this huge wave of money creation. By contrast, the figures for the growth in the U.S. money supply— 18 percent, or a 6.7 annual rate—look subdued. From 1971 to 1973 the U.S., which had been the principal culprit during the 1966–69 period, was no longer the world's engine of inflation. The U.S. had passed the baton to Japan and Europe.

In both periods the same root cause was to blame: Political imperatives forced the central banks to sacrifice the proper objective of monetary policy—control over the money supply for the purpose of providing price stability—in favor of other objectives. In the case of the U.S. from 1966 to 1969 the other objective was the financing of the Vietnam War and the Great Society without any increase in taxes; in the case of Japan and Europe from 1971 to 1973, the other objective was to prevent, delay, or minimize the rise in a country's exchange rate. The pursuit of these "other objectives" led the central banks involved to act in ways that inevitably inflated the money supply, and with equal inevitability, led to serious price inflation.

The excessive amount of international money created during the 1971–73 period can also be measured in terms of U.S. dollar equivalents. In spite of its fall from grace, the U.S. dollar was retained by the world as the currency in which *world prices* for the principal commodities are denominated and traded. It is this global amount of dollar purchasing power that presses against the supply of internationally traded commodities to determine the world price of basic raw materials.

Between year-end 1970 and mid-1973—in just two-and-a-half years— the stock of money issued by Japan and the European group expressed in U.S. dollar equivalents more than doubled! To exacerbate matters, the stock of Eurodollars (liquid liabilities akin to money, denominated in U.S. dollars and held in banks *outside* the United States), which are not included in the totals mentioned above, was expanding at an even faster rate. One does not have to be a disciple of Milton Friedman to believe that this pace of money creation had to lead to a very large if not commensurate increase in the dollar price of traded raw materials. This is exactly what happened.

By the final quarter of 1973 the average rate of inflation in the seven largest market economies of the world plus Switzerland had accelerated to over 12 percent a year, another huge and painful adjustment to powerful monetary imbalances generated by many governments acting in shortsighted concert. Just how much higher that wave of largely monetary inflation was to run after December 1973 is something we will never really know: In that month the course of events was subjected to a second large shock—the curtailment of Arab oil supplies and a quantum jump in the price of petroleum. By the end of 1974 the average rate of inflation in the major economies had quickened to 16.5 percent under the joint pressure of excess money and insufficient oil. What happened next is the subject of the chapter that follows.

FIDDLIN'

Drawing by Chick Larsen
Courtesy *Richmond (Va.) Times-Dispatch*

4

Energy

THE ONSET OF SERIOUS INFLATION and the collapse of the dollar in the early 1970s wounded the postwar economy, but not mortally. The blow that brought the period of fast growth and low inflation to its final close came in the last quarter of 1973. It came in the form of the first oil shock.

Soon after the outbreak of the fourth Arab-Israeli War on Yom Kippur day, October 6, 1973, Saudi Arabia, acting in concert with other oil-exporting Arab states, cut oil production, embargoed sales to the U.S. and the Netherlands, and raised the posted price of its benchmark crude to $11.65 a barrel effective January 1, 1974.* This represented a 350 percent increase over the posted price of $2.59 a barrel that had prevailed just one year earlier.

During 1974, the first full year after that much-larger-than-anticipated increase in the price of the industrial world's most important raw material, the average rate of inflation in the free world's seven largest economies accelerated to 16.5 percent a year. (The seven, in order of size, are the U.S., Japan, West Germany, France, the U.K., Italy, and Canada. Together they accounted for 70 percent of free-world GNP in 1973.) This acceleration took place in spite of the existence of significant government controls over wages and prices in several of these countries.

---

*For an explanation of posted prices and benchmark crude see Note on Oil Pricing on pp. 80–81.

Soon thereafter, all of these economies fell into the most severe recession they had experienced since the 1930s.

A popular explanation of what happened in 1973–74 goes as follows: A cartel called OPEC (the Organization of Petroleum Exporting Countries) had arbitrarily raised the price of oil by a factor of four and a half (i.e., by 350 percent). This massive increase in the price of oil brought about the worldwide inflation of 1974.

A second oil crisis occurred in 1979–80. Revolution in Iran, the second-largest oil-exporting nation, cut Iranian oil production. Iranian exports fell almost to zero in early 1979, thereby reducing the supply of OPEC oil exports by about 15 percent. The shortage of oil that followed caused a large increase in the price of oil on the spot markets.* Other OPEC nations responded by raising the price charged for their oil in quantum jumps. By the end of 1980 Saudi Arabia, the key exporter, had raised the price of its oil from around $12 a barrel—the price that had prevailed since 1974—to $32 a barrel. Other OPEC nations who decided that Saudi pricing policies were too conservative increased the basic contract price* of their oil to $36 a barrel, on top of which they added substantial premiums ranging from $4 to $6 a barrel for quality or proximity to markets.

Once again, world inflation rates accelerated. In the seven largest economies, the average rate of inflation rose from 7½ percent during the year ending December 1978 to 12 percent by year-end 1979. Once again, the large industrial economies, with the notable exception of Japan, fell into recession. And once again the same popular explanations were put forward: A cartel called OPEC had raised oil prices and this in turn had caused worldwide inflation in 1979 and 1980.

The popular explanation for the two most serious economic problems the free world has faced in 40 years—inflation and energy—has interesting implications that should not go unnoticed. First, placing the primary blame for inflation on oil prices and the primary blame for oil prices on OPEC diverts attention from the proposition that our own policies might be the cause of either problem—i.e., the idea that government itself might be the true parent of both the inflation and energy problems. Second, if "outside" forces are to blame, there is little need to face up to the difficult task of restructuring our own policies away from the politically comfortable but economically ruinous direction of the past 15 years.

The trouble with the popular scapegoat explanation is that it is essentially incorrect. As we will see in what follows, the rise in oil prices

*See Note on Oil Pricing, pp. 80–81.

in 1974 and 1979 may have worsened the rate of inflation in those years; it certainly did not create it. Likewise the existence of a cartel called OPEC was not the primary reason for the huge jumps in oil prices that occurred.

Oil and Inflation

The wave of accelerating inflation that peaked in 1974 was well under way before oil prices jumped at the end of 1973. The inflation had its roots in two developments. One development, which we have already discussed, was the vast amount of money creation that occurred prior to mid-1973—a creation that was the direct result of ill-advised monetary policies, first by the U.S. government (1965–69) and later by the governments of other major nations (1971–73). The second development, partly related to the first, was a rapid acceleration in the pace of worldwide industrial activity; by early 1973 this expansion had turned into an industrial superboom of unprecedented scale and speed. For the 12 months ending March 1973, when the rate of acceleration in production crested, industrial activity in the free world's seven largest economies had risen at an average rate of 11.3 percent a year—almost double the average postwar rate prior to 1972, which was already very high. For many industrial materials and industries, including steel and automobiles, the rate of production and demand pressed hard on existing supply capacity. Demand, fueled by rising incomes and the excessive supply of money, put heavy upward pressure on prices. Consequently the rate of inflation accelerated rapidly.

The Pattern of Price Increases

A hundred years ago, the great British economist Alfred Marshall, confronted by the problem of deciding whether demand or cost was the more important factor in determining price, replied by asking, "Which blade of the scissors does the cutting?" The pressure of excessive monetary demand in 1972 and 1973 had to spill over into a commensurate rise in average prices, but just how this *average* rise would be distributed among individual commodities and services depended on supply conditions for each commodity as well as on institutional conditions such as price or wage controls or the existence of long-term contracts within each sector.

Typically, inflation that is brought about by excessive monetary demand will hit raw materials prices first and fastest; the spot markets in which such materials are traded are highly sensitive to current conditions. Next, inflation moves to wholesale prices in general, but here its impact is blunted by the existence of long-term contracts between buyers and sellers. Finally inflation shows up many quarters later at the retail or consumer level, but by now significantly damped down by the fact that slow-to-move items like wages, rents, and utilities comprise a much larger fraction of total retail costs than is true of raw products.

The inflation of 1972–73 followed this generally expected pattern. Spot prices of industrial and agricultural raw materials had been rising rapidly for 18 months *prior* to October 1973. On the London Metal Exchange the dollar prices of copper, lead, zinc, tin, and the precious metals more than doubled between early 1972 and October 1973. Agricultural prices also increased very rapidly, driven in part by huge Soviet purchases of grain that were spurred by serious crop failures in that country. As world inventories of grain and animal feed fell in a world where money was overplentiful, price pressures mounted.

By September 1973, the one-year increase in the index of wholesale prices for the major countries had already reached 18 percent, just about commensurate with the rate at which the world money supply had been expanded prior to mid-1973. In spite of their usual tendency to lag, consumer prices in the seven largest economies had also accelerated rapidly to 9 percent a year by September 1973. It was in this context of already high and accelerating world inflation that oil prices took their quantum leap after October 1973. At most, this jump in oil prices may have exacerbated the world inflation rate in 1974. To argue that it caused the inflation all by itself is farfetched. Our own collective economic policies caused that wave of inflation.

Oil and Inflation, 1973–74

There is a milder version of the oil-push theory of inflation which goes as follows: The large jump in oil prices at the end of 1973 did not *cause* the inflation of 1974, but it was the ineluctable cause of the *acceleration* in the inflation rate in 1974. A look at the evidence on a country-by-country basis does not provide strong support for even this view of the impact that oil prices had.

If it is true that the leap in oil prices was the principal cause of the acceleration of inflation in 1974, we would expect to find that inflation accelerated most in countries that were most dependent on oil imports for their energy supply. The facts do not fully confirm this expectation. In 1974, Japan and Italy, the two countries that were most dependent on oil imports, did suffer large accelerations in their rates of inflation: In 1974 Japan experienced a 90 percent increase in her inflation rate relative to her inflation in 1973; Italy suffered an 80 percent increase.

But how can the same theory explain why Canada, which was a *net oil exporter* in 1973, and the United States, which was the least energy dependent of the other six major industrial countries, also suffered an acceleration of about 75 percent in their inflation rates? Finally, how can the theory explain events in West Germany and Switzerland? Both were heavily dependent on oil imports, yet their inflation rates in 1974 were barely above what they had experienced in 1973.

Surely the oil-push explanation cannot fit all of these behavior patterns. The explanation, or at least a large part of it, lies elsewhere. Both West Germany and Switzerland had moved aggressively to slow their rates of monetary and industrial expansion by early 1973. Indeed, during the last nine months of 1973 they ranked as the two *slowest-growing* economies in the industrial world. This is why their rates of inflation did not accelerate between 1973 (before the oil crisis) and 1974.

In a sense this brings us back to the old dispute between the two opposing schools of thought regarding what determines the behavior of a nation's inflation rate: the theory that inflation is the result of the *pull* of excessive monetary demand and the opposing theory that the *push* of costs is the real culprit. The large increase in oil prices that took place in 1974 provides an important opportunity for testing the validity of the two theories: A common cause (the jump in oil prices) produced some most uncommon effects.

Countries such as Switzerland and West Germany, in which policy had slowed monetary growth rates by mid-1973 and had thereby slowed the pull of demand and expansion, suffered almost no acceleration in inflation in 1974—regardless of their dependence on oil imports. Countries such as Japan, Italy, Canada, and the U.S., in which monetary growth and hence industrial growth rose in 1973, suffered large accelerations in their inflation rates in 1974, again regardless of their quite different degrees of dependence on oil imports.

By and large the evidence supports the view that money and the pull of monetary demand is the critical ingredient in the phenomenon we call inflation. Large jumps in the cost of individual commodities, such as the more than fourfold rise in the cost of oil imports in 1974, are complicating and exacerbating factors, but they do not in themselves determine the overall rate at which prices in general will rise.

Oil and Inflation, 1979–80

The second large jump in oil prices, which took place between year-end 1978 and year-end 1980 (from $12 to $32 a barrel for Saudi Arabian crude), was also associated with a sharp acceleration in world inflation rates. Once again, the sequence of events suggests that the oil prices were not the primary cause of that acceleration.

By early 1979, just before the Iranian revolution caused OPEC oil

Control valve

Drawing by Don Hesse
© 1974 *St. Louis Globe-Democrat*

Note on Oil Pricing

Oil pricing bristles with technicalities. Unfortunately some understanding of these technicalities is essential in order to follow what has happened to the price of oil in international markets.

1. *Posted price.* Prior to 1975, the price of oil was expressed in terms of an official posted price per barrel (42 U.S. gallons). This posted price was not an actual price. It was simply a basis for calculating the host government's revenue per barrel.

For example, on January 1, 1973, the posted price of Saudi Arabian light oil (34° gravity) was $2.591 per barrel. On this the Saudis got the standard royalty of 12½ percent, or $0.324, leaving the operator (in this case ARAMCO) $2.267. Of this, $0.10 was assumed to be the "lifting" or current producing cost per barrel, and the remaining $2.167 was the company's theoretical "profit," on which the Saudi government levied an income tax of 55 percent or $1.192. (The total Saudi "take"—royalties plus taxes—was thus $1.516.) Adding back the estimated $0.10-per-barrel lifting cost, the cash cost to the company was therefore $1.616 a barrel.

Adding an allowance of about $0.50 per barrel to cover the company's return on investment yielded a total cost of $2.116 per barrel for oil delivered on board a tanker in the Persian Gulf. The "landed" cost at a U.S. port (generally in the Gulf of Mexico) would depend on tanker rates or costs. In 1973 these costs ran around $1.50 a barrel, bringing the total landed price to around $3.60 a barrel.

When the Saudis increased their posted price by 350 percent, from $2.591 to $11.651 effective January 1, 1974, they retained the existing pricing system. Their take (royalties plus taxes) increased from $1.516 to $7.00 per barrel. However, assuming no change in tanker rates, the landed price per barrel (at a U.S. Gulf port) of Saudi oil would have increased by only 150 percent, i.e., from $3.60 to $9.10. For all oil imports the U.S. landed price almost tripled (an increase of nearly 200 percent).

2. *Contract price* (post-1975). In December 1974 the traditional pricing system was changed. Posted prices were replaced by a "contract" price at which host countries, who had by now nationalized the oil fields, would sell oil to the operating oil companies. This contract price was the host government's take. Companies accepting contract oil agreed to add only a stipulated markup, i.e., $0.11 a barrel for production expenses and $0.50 a barrel for profit. Thus at a $12.00 contract price, the price at the Persian Gulf port would be $12.61 and the landed price in the U.S. $14.11 (assuming a $1.50 transport cost). Hence, price comparisons between dates prior to and after January 1, 1975, can be quite confusing.

3. *Spot price.* Host countries can elect to take at least their "royalty" oil (i.e., 12½ percent of oil produced under contract) in kind rather than cash. Indeed, in some cases they can also choose to take even more "in kind." This oil can be sold on the spot market (sales not involving long-term contracts) at whatever price the market will bring. On occasions, spot prices (prices at which oil is bought and sold outside the basic long-term contract system) can rise far above contract prices.

4. *Benchmark crude* (sometimes called marker crude). The value of petroleum varies greatly depending on several qualities. The lighter crudes are generally more valuable than the heavier crudes because they can be refined more easily into gasoline. In the complex world of oil prices, the degree of lightness is indicated by a *higher* gravity number, e.g., Libyan (Attifel) crude rated 40° gravity is lighter and more desirable than Saudi Arabian 34° gravity crude, which in turn is lighter than Alaskan 27° gravity crudes. In addition to lightness, low content of sulfur and other impurities and proximity to ultimate markets are also major factors. For Middle Eastern crudes, Saudi Arabian "light" 34° oil loaded on a tanker in the Persian Gulf has become the standard or "benchmark" crude for price setting. The reason is simple. Saudi 34° oil falls about halfway between the very light North African crudes and the very heavy U.S. and Venezuelan varieties. In addition Saudi Arabia is far and away the world's largest oil exporter.

prices to climb far above the level at which they had been stuck for several years, the rate of inflation in the U.S. had already been accelerating rapidly. The rate of increase in the Producer Price Index for finished goods (the new name for the old Wholesale Price Index), which had fallen to 2.7 percent a year in the 12 months ending December 1976, had already accelerated to 10 percent a year in the 12-month period ending February 1979 when the price effect of the second round of OPEC increases first hit our shores. For the Consumer Price Index, the 12-month rate of increase had accelerated from 4.8 percent at year-end 1976 to 10 percent by February 1979.

The rapid rise in oil prices that began in early 1979 did worsen our inflation rate as well as the rate of inflation in other countries. During the first quarter of 1980 the average price of the petroleum we imported had risen to $30 a barrel, double the $15-a-barrel price we paid during the first quarter of 1979. By March 1980 our Consumer Price Index had risen by 14.8 percent over its March 1979 level. Of that (to date) record rate it is estimated that around 2½ points were attributable to oil. The remaining 12 or 13 points of the inflation rate were entirely the result of our own policies.

The outbreak of war between Iraq and Iran in September 1980 led to a substantial cut in oil exports from Iraq, which just prior to that war had ranked as OPEC's second-largest producer. Oil prices continued to rise, but the rate of increase abated for two reasons. Saudi Arabia stepped up its production to over 10 million barrels a day in order to maintain supply to Iraq's former customers, and the onset of another recession in Europe and North America reduced the pressure of world demand for oil. By early 1981, the average barrel of U.S. petroleum imports was costing us $35 as contrasted with $30 a year earlier, but the rate of consumer price inflation, which had been running 14.8 percent during the year ending March 1980, had edged down to 9.5 percent by June 1981.

OPEC and Oil Prices

For most Americans, the energy problem began in the winter of 1974. Motorists had to wait in long lines at gasoline stations. The retail price of their no-longer-freely-available fuel rose by a third, from around 38 cents a gallon in the fall of 1973 to over 50 cents a gallon by March 1974.

The popular explanation for what had happened invariably involved two scapegoats: The OPEC cartel had embargoed oil exports and arbitrarily raised the price of crude petroleum; the large oil companies had exploited the situation in order to fatten their profits. There was not much to be done about the first problem (although a little saber rattling was sporadically heard), so our farsighted leaders in Congress decided to concentrate on the second.

The Arab oil embargo against the U.S. was lifted in March 1974; soon thereafter the lines at gas stations abated and gradually disappeared. By then retail gasoline prices had climbed to a horrifying 55 cents a gallon. "Notice how the shortage disappeared once *they* got the price up?" was the popular way of making a statement by asking a question in those days. The Congress of the United States responded to popular opinion with great speed. Hearings were held in which serious senators in the name of "The American People" demanded to know the facts: Were the large oil and gas companies sitting on shut-in wells loaded with fuel? Were they hoarding production in hidden tanks, abandoned service stations, or, as one rumor had it, in dozens of oil tankers floating loaded to the brim just over the horizon? Even before these investigations ran their full televised course, depletion allowances for oil and gas companies, a once sacrosanct tax provision, were eliminated and three major legislative attempts were made to break up the integrated oil companies by forbidding them to engage in more than any one stage of a four-stage process—exploration and production, transportation, refining, and marketing. When these legislative attempts failed, the Federal Trade Commission was handed the task of achieving the same punitive end, but for just the eight largest companies.

All of this horseplay diverted public attention from the fact that the United States faced a deep and serious energy problem—a problem that had been brewing for more than a decade. The heart of the problem was that U.S. demand for energy was rising far faster than its supply. The principal cause of the problem was a set of U.S. policies, including price and environmental controls, that collectively encouraged the growth in demand for energy and suppressed the growth of supply. We continued to pursue, indeed to intensify, these policies even after tangible signs of our growing energy imbalance began to appear.

By 1973 the rapidly rising imbalance had become so large that something had to give. What gave was the price of OPEC oil, the one factor in the total energy equation over which we had no control. The size of the huge leap in OPEC oil prices in 1973–74 was not attributable to OPEC's power as a cartel; it was an index of how large we had allowed the imbalance to become.

It is true that the price jump in 1973–74 and the second jump in 1979–80 were both triggered by interruptions in OPEC oil supply, but two other facts are more important: Neither interruption was motivated by the cartel's pricing policies, and on both occasions OPEC, the cartel, was a "price follower" not a "price leader." In short, on each occasion

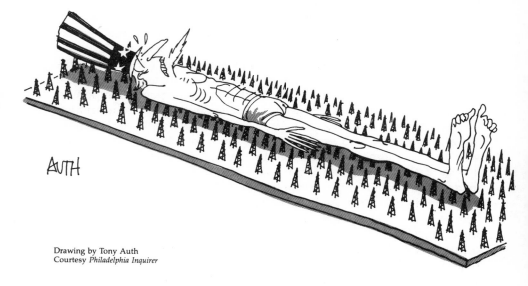

Drawing by Tony Auth
Courtesy *Philadelphia Inquirer*

it was demand and supply that set oil prices—not OPEC. Until the United States understands these brute facts clearly and acts on this understanding, we will not be able to achieve the now crucial objective of getting ourselves out from under the bondage of a seller's market for oil.

The energy problem whose manifestations suddenly appeared in the form of long lines at gas stations in 1974 and reappeared again in 1979 did not spring from the fact that oil-exporting nations were banded together in the form of a cartel. Its roots lay in the fact that our own policies had made us critically dependent on imported oil. These policies began years ago, indeed they began before OPEC itself was born.

Energy in the 1950s

All through the 1950s there existed a buyer's market for oil. Demand was growing rapidly, but supply was growing even faster. The price of oil was weak—indeed it kept falling relative to prices in general. The seven largest international oil companies, known as the "seven sisters,"* were then in almost complete control of production, exports, prices, and hence the revenue that their host countries received per barrel of oil.

*Their current names are Exxon, Mobil, Gulf, Standard of California, Texaco, Shell, and British Petroleum.

The utter weakness of the oil-producing countries was dramatically demonstrated by events in Iran in the early 1950s. Iran was then the largest Middle Eastern oil producer. It tried to rectify matters in its own favor first by nationalizing the Anglo-Iranian Oil Company (now British Petroleum) and then by cutting its oil production almost to zero in order to force a rise in oil prices and an increase in its own revenues. The effort was a hopeless failure. The seven sisters countered these moves by boycotting Iranian oil and by increasing production from other Middle Eastern fields and fields in the U.S. As a result nobody except the militants in Iran even noticed the lost Iranian production. Table 3 tells the story in numbers. It also shows how the U.S. then absolutely dominated the balance between the supply of and demand for free-world petroleum.

Table 3: Oil Production, 1950 and 1952
(millions of barrels a day)

	1950	1952
Iran	0.66	0.02
Saudi Arabia	0.55	0.83
Kuwait	0.33	0.75
Iraq	0.14	0.39
Total of 4	1.68	1.99
U.S.	5.91	6.89

A few years later, in 1956–57 during the second Arab-Israeli War, Egypt seized and closed the European-owned Suez Canal, which at that time was a vital artery for oil traffic. The large oil companies were granted tacit permission by the U.S. government (and its tough antitrust laws) to act together in order to reassign and redeploy the flow of oil to world markets. They did so with such success that few oil users were inconvenienced for long.

As the 1950s drew to a close, there was an excess supply of oil both at home and abroad and oil prices were weak. In 1959 President Eisenhower imposed mandatory controls on oil imports. Henceforth, oil could be imported into the U.S. only under licenses issued by the secretary of the Interior Department. The purpose was to protect domestic producers from "cheap" foreign oil. But like most government interventions into the marketplace, this oil quota system developed an interesting twist. Foreign oil was cheaper (including transport costs) than U.S.-produced oil. Thus each license to import a barrel of oil (known as a "ticket") had an economic value equal to the foreign-domestic price differential. Through the powers it had to "allocate" tickets to refiners in the country, the Department of the Interior soon found itself allocating the equivalent of money. Some small refiners who were routinely granted a larger-than-proportionate share of the total quota found they could make more money by selling their tickets to other refiners than they could by using them to buy and refine petroleum. An active market in tickets began.

This imposition of mandatory barriers to U.S. oil imports further weakened international oil prices. By 1960 prices had fallen by about 15 percent relative to levels that had prevailed in the mid-1950s. The oil-exporting countries were visibly upset. In 1960 the five largest oil-exporting countries—Venezuela, Iran, Iraq, Kuwait, and Saudi Arabia—formed OPEC in order to prevent oil prices from falling, but the cartel was too weak to have any impact on falling prices until the balance of economic power moved into its hands toward the very end of the decade.*

Energy in the 1960s

The pendulum of economic power began to swing the other way in the 1960s. The swing was slow at first, but it accelerated rapidly toward the end of the decade because of an underlying shift in the balance between world oil supply and demand in favor of the oil-exporting countries. What brought about the power shift was the speed at which the economies of the industrial West, and especially the U.S., became dependent on Mideast oil.

During the 1960s the major industrial economies—the U.S., Western Europe, and Japan—grew extremely rapidly. Their use of energy grew even faster than did their economies. On top of this, two phenomena led them to switch out of coal into petroleum and natural gas to supply their burgeoning energy demands: One was the environmental movement, the other was that the price of oil kept falling relative to the price of coal. As a result, world consumption of oil rose very fast. From 1962 to 1972 Western European demand for liquid petroleum measured in millions of barrels per day (mb/d) rose by 170 percent (from 5.3 mb/d to 14.3 mb/d)—all of it from Mideast and African sources. Japanese demand for OPEC oil rose even faster, from 1 mb/d in 1962 to 4.8 mb/d in 1972, a 380 percent increase in ten years.

Energy developments in the U.S. differed in several ways from those in Western Europe and Japan. By 1962 we were already a huge user of

*In the 1960s and 1970s the addition of Algeria, Libya, Nigeria, Indonesia, Ecuador, Qatar, Gabon, and the United Arab Emirates increased OPEC's membership to 13 nations.

oil (some 10 mb/d), but we were also the world's largest producer (some 8 mb/d). We imported less than 20 percent of the oil we used and very little of that came from the Middle East. Although we shifted out of coal in the 1960s, as did Europe and Japan, our principal shift was to domestically produced natural gas, which was then even cheaper than oil because its price was suppressed at artificially low levels by misguided governmental policies.* Total U.S. demand for oil did grow rapidly during the period, but our 60 percent increase from 1962 to 1972 was small compared to the 170 percent increase in Western Europe and the 380 percent increase in Japan. Nonetheless, the U.S. probably had a larger impact on the changing balance of world demand and supply for oil than did any other nation.

The key to the apparent puzzle stated above was the interaction of two facts: the fact that the U.S. was *almost* self-sufficient in oil (we imported only 2 mb/d in 1962) and the fact that our own domestic capacity to produce oil and natural gas was about to reach a peak and then turn down.

From 1962 to 1972, total U.S. consumption of oil rose from 10 mb/d to 16 mb/d; U.S. production rose from 8 mb/d to its peak rate of 11 mb/d in 1970 and then began to edge downward. Thereafter all growth in consumption had to be met either by natural gas or from imports. By 1972 our oil imports had risen to 5 mb/d. In the space of a few years, the world's largest producer of oil had become the world's largest and most rapidly growing importer of oil.

To make matters even worse, U.S. natural gas withdrawals, which had grown very rapidly and thus satisfied the largest part of our total growth in energy demand in the 1950s and 1960s, began to decline sharply after 1970. This added significantly to the growing shortfall of energy that had to be provided by oil imports. In 1973 U.S. imports of crude petroleum, principally from the Middle East and Africa, jumped by 46 percent.

Mere percentages do not capture the huge and sudden impact that the rapidly emerging U.S. dependence on imports had on world oil markets. To appreciate just how large this impact was it is necessary to look at absolute numbers. OPEC production increased at a prodigious rate between 1970 and 1973. Saudi Arabian output more than doubled from 3.5 mb/d to 7.4 mb/d; for all OPEC producers, the annual increase in production averaged nearly 2.5 mb/d. In 1973 the U.S., a relatively new entry into the world market for imported petroleum, increased its

*U.S. government control over the ceiling price of natural gas sold in interstate commerce held that price to well below 17.5 cents per 1,000 cubic feet during the 1960s. This was equivalent to a price of less than $1.00 per barrel of oil at a time when oil in the U.S. was selling for nearly three times that price.

import demand by 1.5 mb/d and thus alone took 60 percent of the available annual increment in supply!

No one in early 1973, not even Israeli military intelligence, could have predicted the timing of the outbreak of another Middle East war on October 6, 1973. But anyone with an eye for trends could have predicted that the exploding U.S. appetite for imported oil was going to create a seller's market for oil by 1974 or at the latest by 1975.

The Road to Crisis, 1970–73

In the early years of the 1970s the turn in the balance of bargaining power between the oil-exporting countries and the oil-importing countries became decisive. One root of that turn, as noted, was the rapidly changing balance between the supply and demand for world oil. The other root was the rapid fall in the relative bargaining power of the seven large international oil companies vis-à-vis governments of the countries in which they produced oil.

Each member country of OPEC had four basic strategies through which it could increase the revenue it received from oil exports:

1. It could raise its rate of production as rapidly as its oil reserves allowed. By and large this was what Saudi Arabia and Iran did between 1967 and 1973.

2. It could ask for an increase in the posted price on which its royalty and tax revenues were based. By and large this did not succeed so long as world output was rising as fast as world demand.

3. It could demand a higher *rate* of tax or royalty. So long as the seven large oil companies held together, such demands would not be met.

4. It could expropriate oil properties, nationalize production, and take its chances on producing and selling oil on its own to world markets. Mexico tried this in the 1930s and Iran in the early 1950s: Both failures were too vivid for this strategy to be followed widely so long as a united group of large oil companies controlled production, technology, financing, and markets.

By the early 1970s, the relative bargaining power of the "seven sisters" had shrunk. It was eroded by a combination of factors:

1. Younger, hungrier oil companies from the U.S., Europe, and Japan began to bid actively for the right to find and extract oil in the Mideast and North Africa. In the process of doing so they gave in rapidly to demands for increased royalties, larger participation by host governments, and higher posted prices.

2. The major oil-exporting nations developed their human resources, people who soon became quite sophisticated about oil technology, mar-

kets, and prices. Indeed, many of these people were educated at our best universities.

3. The leaders of newly installed revolutionary governments—notably in Algeria, Iraq, and Libya—were far more willing to take risks in order to get the increased revenues their ideologies demanded, including the risk of going to the Soviet Union for technology.

4. Our own State Department, for reasons known only to itself, was always more willing to side with the needs of the oil-exporting countries with whom it worked on a daily basis than with the needs of the importing nations—until suddenly the U.S. itself popped up as the world's biggest oil importer!

5. Our own antitrust laws made it increasingly difficult for the seven sisters (five of whom were U.S. corporations) to act in concert.

6. The major thrust of most U.S. governmental policies that had any impact on the energy situation was to increase our dependence on OPEC oil.

Beginning in 1970 the major OPEC countries became increasingly militant in their determination to get larger revenues for their oil. The action began with the revolutionary governments: Algeria nationalized the operations of several American oil companies and forced the remaining French oil concession to raise the posted price of Algerian oil by almost 80 cents a barrel—a huge increase in those days. Libya forced an unprecedented settlement on its oil-producing concessionaire companies, a settlement that not only increased posted prices substantially, but also increased the tax rate applicable to the higher price. In February and March of 1971 the OPEC oil ministers met in Libya, and their concluding resolution, called the Tripoli Agreement (after the city where they met), generalized all and more of these gains for most OPEC producers. In addition the oil producers demanded and received another unprecedented victory—an escalator clause of 2.5 percent a year to compensate them for inflation.

Just as the OPEC countries were ready to settle for these victories, the West inadvertently retaliated by allowing its overall inflation rate to rise to over 10 percent a year (in 1973) and added insult to injury by allowing the exchange value of the dollar (the currency in which oil was priced) to fall substantially on world markets.

The OPEC countries, frustrated and angry, began to press for even higher dollar prices. By mid-1973 the changing supply-demand situation for world oil gave them even more than they had expected. The spot price of oil climbed to above the negotiated posted prices. The reason, outlined earlier, was by now obvious to anybody who looked at trends in demand and supply. In June 1973, the more radical members of OPEC began to press harder for even higher prices and revenues. For example, Iraq wanted to scrap the Tripoli Agreement and its 2.5-percent-a-year escalation clause and shift to a policy whereby each country could unilaterally set its own price. Iraq's major move to abrogate existing contracts failed, but OPEC as a body did manage to agree that the 2.5-percent-a-year escalation clause was no longer adequate in a world of 10 percent inflation.

Over the next few months even the moderate OPEC countries such as Saudi Arabia and Kuwait began to get militant as they discovered that the free-market or spot price for oil was rising above contract prices which until only recently they had regarded as representing a stupendous increase. By September 1973 all OPEC countries decided that it was time to call yet another meeting in October to decide on yet another escalation in contract prices. Just two days before the meeting began in Vienna, the Arab-Israeli war broke out on October 6. Soon after that the price of oil as an economic issue was replaced by the far more powerful concept of oil as a political weapon.

War, Embargo, and Prices

On October 16, 1973, while the OPEC ministers were still at the Vienna meeting, another meeting was called in Kuwait. This one included the oil ministers of only the Arab OPEC nations. They quickly issued a communiqué that expressed their *binding* decision to cut their oil exports by at least 5 percent a month, every month, until Israel completely withdrew from Arab territories it had occupied in the 1967 war. In addition, oil exports to the U.S. and the Netherlands were embargoed because of their "unfriendly" attitude to the Arabs. The Arab states, save Iraq, voted unanimously for these decisions. Iraq abstained because it felt that the motions had not gone far enough.

The important fact here was that Saudi Arabia, the key producing country, which had previously resisted the use of oil as a political weapon, actually spearheaded the actions taken at Kuwait. Indeed the Saudis went further: A few weeks later they decided to cut their own production by 10 percent a month rather than the minimum 5 percent enjoined by the vote at the Kuwait meeting. At the same time they tightened the wording of their resolution to make sure that oil would not slip through to the U.S. via indirect channels. On November 4, 1973, at a second meeting in Kuwait, the Arab oil ministers agreed that they would all cut November 1973 production by 25 percent from the September 1973 level to be followed by *further* cuts of 5 percent a month until their stated political demands were met.

By December the Saudis had induced the U.S. to act as a mediator in the war. In January 1974, Egyptian President Anwar Sadat himself pressed the Arabs for an early end to the boycott in order to facilitate the Egyptian-Israeli disengagement agreement that had been arranged under U.S. auspices. By March 1974 both the production cuts and the embargo were lifted. But the events of late 1973 marked a change in economic relationships—a change whose economic effects will last for decades.

The Vienna meeting of OPEC ministers in October 1973 at which higher prices had been requested had been adjourned to allow the oil companies to return to their headquarters for "consultation." But even before those company representatives returned to Vienna, OPEC decided it would unilaterally post its own prices, thus completing once and for all the takeover by their governments of control over their oil revenues. The posted price of Saudi benchmark crude was increased by 70 percent to $5.12 per barrel.

Two years earlier a request for an increase of such a magnitude would have been regarded as an outrage. In the context of late 1973, it was a joke. After the politically inspired oil embargoes and production cuts began, the spot-market price of oil began to climb sharply. By December 1973, bidding for Iranian oil on the open market reached $16 per barrel. A month or two later there were reports that independent buyers were offering more than $20 a barrel for Libyan and Nigerian crudes. The posted price of $5.12 established at the OPEC meeting in October 1973 was obsolete even before it was promulgated.

Naturally the ministers had to meet again. They convened on December 22–23 in Teheran. There, mixing a new sense of power with reality, they decided that the long-term posted price of benchmark oil should be raised to $11.65 a barrel. The $11.65 price for Saudi oil established in January 1974 (the corresponding prices for Nigerian and Libyan oils were $14.69 and $15.77 a barrel) was a compromise. The Saudis wanted a lower price; the hawks, including the Shah of Iran, thought the price should be higher. The West did not know what to think: Relieved to see the political-military crisis pass and Mideast oil exports flowing again, most observers did not dwell on the economic implications of what had happened. The few who did quickly realized their enormity: OPEC had increased the world's bill for imported oil by $75 billion a year—from $33 billion in 1973 to $108 billion in 1974. This increase was equivalent to a new "tax" of about 2.5 percent of the combined GNP of the world's principal industrial countries on whom it was imposed.

U.S. Energy Policies Prior to 1973

Some observers believe that the U.S. had to face an energy problem in 1973 because it did not, as a nation, have an "energy policy." This is partly correct, but also partly misleading. We had a whole set of policies affecting energy. The trouble was that these policies were put in place to achieve objectives that had little to do with the most important issue of any energy policy—the balancing of energy supply and demand. In fact, the result of our policies had been to create a growing imbalance between demand and supply. As I heard a lecturer quip many years ago, "The thrust of U.S. policies on energy is to make us critically dependent on Mideast oil, and the thrust of U.S. foreign policy is to make sure we don't get it!"

Among the many mistaken policies that made the first half of his forecast come true, one stands out as a blunder of historic proportions: This was the Supreme Court *Phillips* decision in 1954 requiring the Federal Power Commission (FPC) to control the wellhead price of natural gas sold in interstate commerce.

Natural Gas

Before World War II, natural gas, which was then generally found as a by-product in the search for oil, had little or no commercial value. Frequently, it was a dangerous nuisance that had to be flared at the wellhead.

The development of large diameter long-distance gas pipelines during World War II converted this ugly stepchild into a potential Cinderella. Gas could heat homes, fuel factories, and spin utility turbines in the big urban centers with far less pollution and at far lower expense than could rival fuels such as coal and oil. The gas that had been found in Texas and Louisiana as a by-product of oil suddenly became valuable. Producers began to search actively for natural gas itself. With the rapid rise in demand, the price that producers charged for gas also rose.

The pipelines and utilities that purchased gas in growing quantities for resale to their customers began to object to higher gas prices at the wellhead, even though gas was far less expensive than substitute fuels. The issue of wellhead gas prices became a political football. Consumer states wanted federal price regulation; producing states did not.

In 1938, the Federal Power Commission had been given permission to regulate the rates that the handful of interstate gas pipelines then in existence could charge for transporting gas. After World War II some consumerists in the FPC were anxious to extend their power to cover regulation of gas prices at the wellhead. But pipelines, like local utilities, are franchised monopolies whose prices have to be regulated. By contrast, natural gas was produced by thousands of companies in a highly competitive market.

LEADER OF THE FREE WORLD

©1979 HERBLOCK

Drawing by Herblock
© 1979 Herblock in *The Washington Post*

The Issue of Price Regulation

Congress was bitterly divided over the issue of barring or granting the FPC jurisdiction over wellhead prices. It finally came down on the side of legislating a free market for wellhead gas. There was in fact no precedent for regulating the price of a commodity just because it is sold to a regulated utility—otherwise, for example, we would have to regulate the price of virtually everything a regulated telephone company buys! But the real issue was no longer a question of logic or economics—it had become a question affecting our emerging political obsession, the redistribution of income. Rising gas prices would transfer income from consumers to producers; price control would prevent such a transfer. Predictably President Truman vetoed the bill exempting gas from FPC control. The question of whether the FPC did or did not have control over producer prices then went to the Supreme Court. The Court unabashedly decided to play Robin Hood. It instructed the FPC to proceed with price regulation.

The FPC Decision

After grappling for years with the impossible problem of setting prices for thousands of individual gas producers, the FPC, which had by now become a large and very consumerist agency, decided to regulate prices not for individual companies but for large geographic areas. Its first decision in the early 1960s set the ceiling price of gas at around 15 cents per mcf (thousand cubic feet). On an energy equivalent basis this price equates to a price of 87 cents a barrel for low sulfur oil or about 2 cents a gallon. The producers argued that this was not regulation but price suppression with a vengeance. Their lawyers and witnesses were able to argue their case in court because ours is a constitutional democracy, but their arguments got nowhere. By 1970 the nominal ceiling price allowed, already set too low in 1960, had inched up by only 15 percent, that is, at half the rate of general inflation.

The outstanding feature of the long debates in Congress, in the courts, and in the FPC hearing rooms was that no one raised the relevant question: What will the imposition of price control do to the future balance between the demand and supply of U.S. energy?

The Consequences of Gas Price Regulation

Suppressing the price of a commodity below its proper market value has predictable consequences: It stimulates use (demand), discourages supply, and sooner or later leads to shortages. This is exactly what happened. For a commodity such as energy, tracing these consequences is complicated by the fact that very long time lags are involved.

In the case of natural gas there were several reasons for the lag. The Supreme Court's decision, rendered in 1954, did not have an immediate impact because there was considerable hope that it would be reversed by Congress. President Eisenhower did immediately seek to annul the Court's ruling by legislation. The bill to exempt the price of wellhead gas from FPC control cleared Congress after a bitter floor fight. Just as it did, evidence appeared that an oil company's lawyer had tried to bribe one of the key senators involved in the passage of the bill. The president reluctantly vetoed the bill on the grounds that "any good bill ought to be passed without having a terrible stench connected with it."

There was then a further lag attributable to the lingering hope that the FPC, now fully empowered to regulate the ceiling price of natural gas at the wellhead, would do so fairly and intelligently, or be forced to do so by the courts. It took several years for that hope to evaporate. The economic effects of regulation began only after the first FPC trial and decision in 1962. The level of drilling activity to find new gas, which had more than doubled between 1950 and 1960, began to fall. Thereafter the gas timetable went as follows:

1960   Natural gas price regulation begins. Exploration and drilling begin to fall.

1960–67   Reserves continue to increase but at a slower and slower pace.

1967–72   Reserves actually fall as we withdraw more than we find. We are living high by selling the furniture!

1973   Our diminishing ability to withdraw from depleting reserves leads to a fall in annual production. Large shortages of gas appear, as the demand for gas keeps expanding very rapidly because the regulated price of gas is still suppressed far below its market value: In a world of $12-a-barrel oil the FPC was still mandating that gas was worth at most the equivalent of $1.30 a barrel!

The Development of Imbalance

Between 1950 and 1960, before gas price regulation was put into effect, producer prices for gas doubled; the annual number of exploratory gas wells drilled also doubled; gas production (withdrawals) doubled; gas consumption doubled; and our established inventory of gas reserves *rose* by the equivalent of 13 billion barrels of oil (see Note on Energy Equivalents; all reserve figures exclude Alaskan gas). The increase in annual gas production between 1950 and 1960 took care of two-thirds of our annual increase in total energy use—from the equivalent of 16 mb/d in 1950 to 21 mb/d in 1960. Over this period oil imports rose only modestly, from 0.5 mb/d to 1.6 mb/d.

After 1960 the picture began to change. Natural gas prices, now controlled, rose by only 15 percent between 1960 and 1970, far less than the rate of general inflation; the number of exploratory gas wells drilled annually *fell* by one-half; gas consumption, spurred by the bargain prices at which gas was available, continued to double; gas withdrawals (production), now also subject to regulatory controls over production rates, also almost doubled. But after the middle of the decade the rise in annual withdrawals was coming out of inventories (reserves). From 1967 to 1970 these inventories fell by the equivalent of 5 billion barrels of oil.

Between 1960 and 1970 as energy consumption increased rapidly, gas was still an important energy provider. Annual energy consumption rose from the equivalent of 21 mb/d in 1960 to 32 mb/d in 1970. Of this huge 11 mb/d increase nearly 40 percent was met from higher gas production. But part of the increased pressure of demand spilled over to imports. In spite of mandatory quotas, the volume of oil imports doubled from 1.6 mb/d in 1960 to 3.2 mb/d in 1970. This doubling was significant because the U.S. was no longer just a trivial importer of oil: We had by 1970 become the world's second-largest importer, next only to Japan.

The Imbalance Goes Exponential

The handwriting was on the wall by 1970. It was clear for everybody to read except for those who would not look. Domestic oil production had already begun to fall and was predictably going to fall further. Our domestic gas production was at the physical limit of the rate at which gas could be withdrawn from a now rapidly shrinking reservoir. Gas shortages and interruptions began to appear. At the same time, the increased use of coal and uranium was being bitterly fought and successfully obstructed by a strong environmental lobby, as was our use of the Alaskan oil and gas we had found. In the entire energy equation only the demand side was rising. Indeed the rise was accelerating as *real* gas prices (i.e., gas prices relative to all other prices) were further reduced by mindless regulation.

There was only one feasible place the U.S. could turn to for the increased energy it was demanding in the face of static or declining domestic supplies, and that was oil imports. In a mere three years, between 1970 and 1973, U.S. demand for imported oil doubled again. As we went from 3.2 mb/d of imports in 1970 to 6.5 mb/d by mid-1973, we became not only the world's fastest-growing importer but passed Japan to become the world's largest importer as well. At the rate we were going, the U.S. alone would have needed almost all of OPEC's production by 1980.

The developments were ominous, but in mid-1973 who cared? Gasoline was available, on demand, price controlled at 37.9 cents a gallon including taxes; the automobile industry was selling its domestic makes at the fastest rate on record (a record that still stands), their already poor fuel performance further worsened by the elaborate government-imposed antipollution and safety requirements. Natural gas, our most important domestic source of energy, was still price controlled in 1973 at the absurdly low equivalent of 3 cents a gallon of oil. The caribou in Alaska could still wander from east to west or vice versa without having to go under or over any pipelines. Given the imbalance in supply and demand, the events of December 1973 were almost inevitable. And it was also almost inevitable that the politicians and the regulators put the entire blame on OPEC and the oil companies.

Government and Energy, 1973–80

The policies required to bring energy demand and energy supply into better balance had two components—increased supply and reduced demand. The simplest approach to both components would have been to deregulate the price of natural gas and oil and, consistent with other national priorities, to abolish the mess of tangled governmental regulations over matters affecting energy. Needless to say this was not done.

But in the heat of the impending crisis a few moves in the correct direction were made.

Nixon

In September 1973, just before the crisis struck, President Nixon pleaded with the Congress to approve the trans-Alaska pipeline which had been held up by environmentalists for four years after the large discovery of North Slope oil. Congress did act positively on this request in November. It also acted on two other, less important fronts—imposing a nationwide 55 mile-per-hour speed limit and year-round daylight saving time.

Another positive move that was made during the Nixon years was the streamlining of the maze of bureaucratic responsibility for energy matters. Prior to 1973, a large number of federal agencies, frequently working at cross purposes with one another, exercised jurisdiction over segments of the overall energy equation. Each bureaucratic bailiwick had its counterpart in some congressional committee. Such an arrangement virtually guaranteed the absence of a coherent energy policy. The problem became worse after the passage of the Clean Air Act of 1970 and the creation of the Environmental Protection Agency (EPA). The EPA soon had its finger in every corner of the energy pie. Virtually everything it did served either to reduce supply or increase the demand for oil and gas and thus worsen the imbalance. As someone once cracked, OPEC's best friend in the United States government was not the State Department, it was the EPA. In December 1973, the Federal Energy Office was established with broad authority over national energy policy. The creation of a single energy "czar" within the executive branch did offer the promise of a more coherent basis for policy.

The positive steps taken to improve energy policy were offset by a number of negative actions. Whereas before 1971 the president had been leaning toward the idea of asking the Congress to deregulate natural gas prices, in 1973 when general price controls began to be lifted, he responded to strong political pressures and requested that controls be retained on oil prices. Later, he added mandatory allocation regulations to price controls. The result, to put it mildly, was a bureaucratic nightmare that remained in effect until 1981 when President Reagan abolished all price controls on oil.

Under the system of oil price controls that were in effect from 1971 to 1981, the same commodity, oil, was subject to dozens of different prices, depending upon the category to which a particular barrel of oil was bureaucratically assigned. There was old oil and new oil, lower-tier oil, upper-tier oil,* oil from stripper wells (less than 10 barrels a day production), Alaskan oil, and oil from. wells in what is known as Naval Petroleum Reserves. The prices set ranged from a low of $5.25 a barrel for old oil to a high that was equal to the full price of imported oil, then around $12 a barrel. The average price ceiling on domestic oil was $8.75. Sometimes companies did not know the exact mix of categories that flowed into or out of the network of pipelines through which crude oil is transported.

The purpose of price control was twofold: to minimize the impact of the rising cost of imported oil on the consumer and to minimize the profitability of domestic oil production. This might have been good social policy, but like most price controls that suppress the price of a product below its equilibrium level, it was bad economic policy. It simply made demand higher and supply lower than either would have been under a free-market pricing system, thus further worsening our already large energy imbalance.

From OPEC's point of view the imposition of price controls on domestic U.S. oil must have been a most welcome development. One fear that any cartel faces is that the price increase which it imposes will bring about an enduring reduction in the demand for the product it sells. By intervening in order to hold down *average* prices the consumer had to pay for oil, the U.S. government was in effect shielding OPEC from a portion of the adverse consequences the cartel might otherwise suffer each time it raised its own prices.

The 1973 move to continue oil price controls after other price controls were lifted was not the only piece of energy legislation we passed in the 1970s that deserved the stamp "OPEC Relief Act." It is a general rule that one bad regulation invariably leads to the need for more bad regulations. The inconsistent system of control over domestic oil prices in 1974 was no exception. Its inevitable sequel was soon to follow.

Politicians and bureaucrats love few things better than handing out pieces of paper that entitle recipients to something of value to which those recipients were not previously entitled. Since neither congressmen nor bureaucrats produce the property they transfer, the cost has to come out of someone else's pocket.

As discussed earlier, the imposition of mandatory oil import quotas in 1959 created governmental handouts called "tickets" which gave holders the right to import the then less-expensive foreign oil. In the interest of social justice and possibly of incremental votes, these tickets were delib-

---

*For any producing well, monthly production up to the average 1975 volume was classified as "lower tier" and was allowed a lower price; production above that level was classified as "upper tier" and commanded a different, higher price.

erately overallocated to small refiners of oil and underallocated to large refiners. The former routinely sold them to the latter at a price that was just about equal to the difference between the higher domestic price of crude and the lower price of imported oil.

In 1974 the situation turned into the exact reverse of what it had been. The controlled price of domestic oil was suddenly much lower than the price of imported oil. Companies that owned access to domestically produced oil were thus at an advantage relative to those who had less access and thus had to use expensive imported oil. The federal government invented an "entitlements" program to rectify this situation. Under this program, no one could refine a barrel of price-controlled domestic oil without a governmental "entitlement" to do so. Like the tickets they replaced, such entitlements (each equivalent to one barrel of oil) were handed out by governmental agencies under the watchful eye of the Congress. The general idea was that everybody should have theoretical access to the *same* proportion of price-controlled oil regardless of whether they produced it or not. Because the price of old domestic oil had been set at $5.25 a barrel in a world of $12-a-barrel oil, the value of each entitlement rose quickly to $6.75 a barrel. Companies that produced price-controlled oil had to buy a $6.75-a-barrel entitlement from some other company in order to refine any of their own old oil in excess of a stipulated amount. Small refiners who had little or no oil were paid $6.75 per barrel of entitlement by companies who had oil but no entitlements. Again, the results of the program were predictable. Many good minds were turned from the search for new oil reserves to the search for entitlements. In addition two new constituencies were added to the groups that already advocated a continuation of price controls: the direct beneficiaries of the entitlements program and the platoons of bureaucrats who administered and litigated its intricacies at taxpayer's expense. Strangely enough, the income-redistribution effects of the program itself were perverse. The average recipient of entitlements who happened to be favored by the program was a lot richer than the average worker who had an interest in the oil-producing companies through his or her pension fund.

Ford

The centralized apparatus for formulating national energy policy within the executive branch that had been set up in 1973 made it possible for President Ford to submit a well-formulated and truly comprehensive energy program in December 1974, just a few months after he had been sworn in as president. The Ford program asked the Congress to deregulate the price of natural gas and oil and to restore a free market in energy in order to reduce our still-growing energy imbalance. It also asked Congress to temper the zeal of the Clean Air Act in order to encourage the necessary switch from natural gas and oil to coal. On top of this it had the courage to ask for a $3-per-barrel tariff on all imported oil in order to curb demand. It was a coherent, consistent, and sensible set of policy decisions aimed at the heart of the energy problem. Unfortunately it was not accepted by Congress. In place of the solution that the program offered, Congress decided to pursue scapegoats of its own making. Instead of decontrolling prices (with or without a tax on excess profits) Congress decided to lower the price of controlled domestic oil by 15 percent. This blatantly political step encouraged demand, suppressed supply, and accelerated our growing reliance on imported oil. Incidentally, it also increased the price of each barrel of "entitlement" by about one dollar.

Carter

Energy was not a major issue in the presidential campaign of 1976, but President-elect Carter had obviously planned on presenting a comprehensive energy package to the Congress soon after he took office. He did so in April 1977, three months after he was inaugurated. In his televised message, he declared the "Moral Equivalent of War" on the energy problem. Like much of what he did, his program mixed good and bad in equal proportion. The principal element in the Carter program was that the price of oil to the consumer would be raised to the level dictated by world oil prices. However, the price to the producer was to be held at its previous controlled level. The difference, dubbed the "crude oil equalization tax," would go to the government to be "rebated" to the public in the form of tax credits. In addition, there were 112 other proposals, including a proposal to decontrol natural gas prices over a seven-year span. The main thrusts of the Carter energy plan were to let higher prices blunt demand, to give the government a huge tax increase which it could reallocate to the public, and to outlaw any financial incentive to producers.

The trouble with the program lay in its unstipulated "rebate" formula. If, as a consequence of deregulation, people would get back in tax rebates *exactly* the extra amount they were going to have to pay for uncontrolled energy, the program was at best redundant: It would not change a single thing on either side of the demand-supply equation. If, on the other hand, the government was going to be left free to use the proceeds of the huge crude oil equalization tax that was proposed, the idea could no longer pose as an energy program: It was simply a license for yet another massive wealth-redistribution effort. Puzzled by the ambiguities of the president's "Moral Equivalent of War"—which cartoonists had translated into the feline-sounding acronym MEOW—the Congress decided to shelve the entire matter for a year and a half. In November 1978 President Carter finally got his energy bill. Except for the phased seven-year timetable for the gradual deregulation of natural gas prices, it bore little resemblance to what he had proposed. Nonetheless, the deregulation of gas was a constructive step of major importance.

After the Iranian revolution in 1979 caused the price of OPEC oil to take another quantum jump and gasoline lines started forming again in the U.S., President Carter announced his intention to deregulate the price of oil—a "painful" step as he called it, but a necessary one. The suggested decontrol was to be subject to a large 50 percent "windfall" profits tax over and above normal income taxes on oil company earnings. Actually it was a tax on production and not on profits. The proceeds were to go to help poor families pay for their fuel, to increase subsidies for mass transit, and to create a new governmental fund called the "energy security fund." Months later Congress voted in the two major elements of the program—the windfall profits tax and a phased-in decontrol of oil prices—but left out the frills. It was another late, but constructive, step. At long last, the giant American economy, reared on decades of cheap and abundant energy, was told that it should begin its painful adaptation to a world of scarce and expensive oil.

The Response of Energy Demand and Supply

Prices play a critical role in a market economy: They serve to balance supply and demand. By artificially suppressing the price of natural gas in the 1960s and the price of both gas and oil in the 1970s, the government had brought about a growing imbalance in the U.S. market for energy.

The original reasons for imposing price controls on natural gas were essentially political. The idea was to benefit consumers at the expense of producers. The subsequent reluctance to let the forces of the marketplace correct the obvious imbalance that developed after 1970 was also essentially political, but it was given the veneer of an economic rationale through two theorems invented in Washington:

1. The U.S. could not or would not respond to an increase in the controlled price of gas and oil by curbing consumption. All that price decontrol would do was place an extra financial burden on consumers.

2. U.S. producers would not respond to higher prices (and hence higher profits) by increasing their search for gas and oil. As some politicians suggested, they would simply use their "obscene" oil-gotten profits to "buy department stores." What is more, even if they did increase

the rate of investment in exploration and drilling, there were no significant deposits of oil and gas left to be found.

The controls over our two largest domestic sources of energy provided only temporary protection for the U.S. consumer. Their longer-run effect was to create conditions in which the countries that supplied our rising tide of imported oil raised prices by far more than they could have done had domestic oil and gas prices not been controlled.

The futility of our policy soon became apparent. Our bill for imported oil rose from $3 billion a year in 1970 to nearly $30 billion in 1974 and to $48 billion in 1977. Had our policy of inaction not been reversed, our oil bill for 1980 would have exceeded $150 billion, equal to 70 percent of our total earnings from exports—a drain we could not have sustained for long.

To some people in Washington the solution to the serious problems created by existing energy regulation was the imposition of even more regulations. To them the only equitable answer was for the U.S. to limit oil imports via government controls and then to spread the predictable shortage that would ensue by mandatory rationing of oil and gas. Fortunately policy did not take this turn. Instead it moved, albeit timidly and cautiously, toward allowing a freer play of market forces in order to restore a better balance between demand and supply.

When it became clear around 1978 that oil and gas prices were going to be freed and thus rise toward world market levels, the process of adjustment began in earnest. And once begun, it moved far more swiftly than the original and continuing proponents of governmental control had either predicted or envisioned.

From 1970 to 1977 the volume of petroleum imported into the U.S. (a measure of our imbalance) had more than tripled. In 1971 when then President Nixon delivered his energy message to Congress, we were importing 3 million barrels per day. In 1974, after the first oil crisis, when then President Ford delivered his urgent energy message to Congress, we were importing 6.6 mb/d. By the first quarter of 1977 when then President Carter declared the moral equivalent of war on the problem of rising oil imports, they had climbed to 9.5 mb/d. Thereafter, as it became clear that the government was going to remove its visible thumb from the marketplace, the rapid climb in oil imports was not only stopped—it was reversed. By the second quarter of 1981 oil imports were down to 5.5 mb/d.

Demand

The adaptation of demand to price takes place through several different processes. The initial impact of the new policies, i.e., the intent of the government finally to let prices of domestic oil and gas rise to the levels set by OPEC, was to persuade the U.S. to reduce the rate at which it ran its huge stock of energy-using machines. We cut down on our driving, our heating, our cooling, and the pace at which we utilized industrial equipment per unit of production.

The second and more important impact was to persuade us to amend or replace our stock of energy-using equipment with energy conservation in mind: Houses and factories were insulated, energy-inefficient equipment was scrapped, and gradually new and more energy-efficient forms of capital were installed—machines, cars, trucks, planes, and structures. U.S. automobile manufacturers, pushed by foreign competition, joined the party by placing miles per gallon (MPG) at the very top of their list of sales appeals, but this began in late 1978 only after they were thoroughly convinced that the government's policy of suppressing oil prices had indeed changed. As a result the average car sold in 1979 was designed to be twice as fuel-efficient as the 1969 gas guzzler it replaced, and so on year after year. It will take about ten years (the average life of a car) to complete the first phase of this process—the total replacement of an old fleet of cars built with little thought regarding fuel efficiency with the first generation of cars designed explicitly for fuel efficiency. The same kind of change took place with regard to airplanes and industrial machinery.

The third and most important signal of adaptation was the start of a shift to less energy-intensive life-styles. Thousands of changes in the architecture and design of offices, factories, homes, and swimming pools joined with thousands of changes in patterns of living, work, and vacations to reduce our future need for imported oil. In the eight-year period from 1965 to 1973 the nation's use of energy grew by over 40 percent. In the eight years between 1973 and 1981 the growth in U.S. energy use fell to zero. This occurred in spite of the fact that U.S. adaptation to domestic oil and gas price decontrol did not begin in earnest until 1978.

In 1973, when total free-world consumption of oil was close to 50 mb/d (of which the U.S. used more than one-third), the generally accepted prediction was that by 1980 free-world consumption would rise to 110 mb/d. The big leap in oil prices that occurred at the end of 1973 changed that scenario drastically. By 1981 free-world oil consumption had not doubled; it was down to only 48 mb/d, actually lower than it had been in 1973.

Supply

The supply side of the oil equation responded to the removal of controls as rapidly as the demand side did. Exploration and drilling for oil and gas rose sharply. Indeed, such activity not only reversed the large decline it experienced in the 1960s and early 1970s, it rose so rapidly that in 1980 new drilling records were established. Contrary to the pessimistic bureaucratic assumption that underpinned the case for continued price control, the new exploration activity was successful. In 1980, the steep plunge that had been taking place in proven oil and gas reserves was reversed: We actually found more hydrocarbons than we withdrew.

Outside the U.S. the high prices for energy after 1973 had an equally stimulating effect on oil and gas production—notably in Mexico and the North Sea but also to a lesser degree in many other areas around the globe.

Substitutes for oil and natural gas were also explored and produced, ranging from windmills and solar energy to the burning of garbage, alcohol, and coal. Only in one arena of future energy supply was there a large policy setback. That was in the arena of nuclear-powered electricity. The sharp rise of both rational and irrational worries regarding the economy and safety of this route to lower dependence on OPEC's oil led to a sharp decrease in the orders for new nuclear reactors. By 1979 the number of new orders for reactors in the U.S. was down to zero. But this adverse development was overwhelmed by the combination of the other developments.

By early 1981 the demand-supply equation had changed dramatically. OPEC production, which had risen by nearly 50 percent from 1969 to 1974, had fallen by over 25 percent between 1974 and early 1981. Nonetheless in mid-1981 there were no lines at gasoline stations—indeed there was (at least temporarily) a *glut* of oil, something that had been almost unimaginable just two years earlier. In mid-1981 oil prices actually began to *fall*. Between December 1980 and September 1981, the weighted average price of OPEC oil exports fell from $35.50 a barrel to $33.50, a price decrease of about 6 percent.

*"Gosh, how I envy you the future, son. Almost my whole life
has been lived in a Keynesian context."*

5

Government and the Economy

BY 1973–74 BOTH INFLATION AND ENERGY had grown to national problems of menacing proportions. Their joint weight depressed the economy's capacity to produce goods and services; even worse, it reduced our already declining rate of productivity growth almost to zero. In the 1960s, growth in output per worker had averaged 2.5 percent *a year*; after 1973 it took the full *seven years* to the end of the decade for the economy to achieve a total increase of just 2.5 percent in output per worker.

In 1973 what the economy needed from its national government was a cogent program that would give the highest priority to three national objectives:

1. The eradication of inflation and its causes.
2. The reduction of our dependence on OPEC oil.
3. The elimination of barriers to productivity growth.

The crisis of 1973–74 provided an ideal opportunity for a bold program to achieve these objectives. What we got from our government for the rest of the decade fell miserably short of what was needed.

Washington in 1973 was unusually ill-prepared for the challenge it faced. The Congress had become an undisciplined collection of conflicting fiefdoms, each with its own set of special interests—a body which had accumulated so many parochial priorities that it behaved as if it were unable to pursue any genuine national priority. Presidential leadership—the ability to see clearly what the one or two critical national priorities are and to mobilize the people and the Congress to act on them—simply did not exist. The first postcrisis president was already mired in Watergate before the oil crisis struck; the second, a caretaker president, faced the overwhelming political opposition that had been elected in the aftermath of Watergate itself; the third was unable to lead because he was personally locked in to almost as large and undisciplined a collection of conflicting parochial priorities as the Congress he was supposed to lead.

Seven Grasshopper Years

After the first oil crisis, seven years went by without a serious assault on the economy's three most important problems—inflation, energy, and productivity. In 1979 the bells tolled again for a second time, this time even louder.

In 1977 and 1978, our energy imbalance, measured by our need to import oil, was 50 percent higher than the already high 1973 level that had unleashed the first oil crisis.* In 1979–80 the price of imported oil escalated again, to $35.50 a barrel by the end of 1980, nearly three times the $12-a-barrel price that should have alarmed us into taking serious action in 1974. By early 1980 the rate of inflation measured over a 12-month span had climbed to 15 percent. At the same time the annual gain achieved in output per worker had fallen to below zero.

It was becoming increasingly clear by 1980 that inflation, energy, and productivity were not the only important national problems facing us: There was a fourth problem, the problem of the national government itself—a government whose size and scope had grown to gigantic proportions; whose budget kept on rising rapidly because of a continuing inflation that was itself fueled in part by the rapidly rising budget; whose massive and rising intake of taxes and output of regulations stifled the economy on which it fed; whose extensive political agenda kept getting in its own way every time it tried to turn its course in order to adapt the economy to a rapidly changing world.

The largest cost to society of this gigantism was not just the rising share of the national income it demanded, nor the large drag it placed on economic growth, nor even the potential threat to individual freedom it posed; the real cost was that government's gigantism had produced

*Between 1973 and 1978 every other major economy had *reduced* its demand for oil imports; their average reduction in the volume of oil imports was 15 percent.

an inertia that prevented it from doing the essential things that only governments can do.

In any case, the years from 1973 to 1980—when much could have been done to correct the basic imbalances within the economy in order to clear the way for a renewal of noninflationary growth in the 1980s— were essentially wasted. Essentially, but not entirely. Winston Churchill once said that he could always count on the U.S. to do the right thing— but only after it had first tried every possible wrong alternative. From 1973 to 1980 we tried a large number of wrong alternatives and in the process gradually and partially stumbled toward a number of correct solutions regarding energy and inflation.

The deep and interrelated problems the economy faced in 1980 were becoming too urgent to be left to the mercy of a random stumbling from one expediency to the next. By 1980, policy formulation had reached an inescapable turning point. Government's power over the private economy had to be shifted decisively in either one of two directions. Policy could turn toward a coherent and effective set of direct controls over prices, wages, and resource allocation. Alternatively, it could turn in the opposite direction, toward a significant reduction in governmental intervention in the marketplace. One thing was certain by 1980: It could no longer keep on vacillating between the two. For the third time in its history the U.S. was forced by circumstances to face the task of redefining the optimal relationship between the state and the economy it was supposed to serve.

Ideas and Events

As we have discussed, there are trends in economic ideas just as there are trends in economic events, and watersheds between the trends that seem to determine how both ideas and events will flow into the future. So far as the relationship of the state to the economy is concerned, there have thus far been three watershed years in modern times—each associated with the name of a great economic philosopher—Adam Smith, 1776; Karl Marx, 1848; John Maynard Keynes, 1936.*

The middle date, 1848, the year Marx's *Communist Manifesto* was published, is a critical one largely for that extensive continental arc of Eurasia which runs from Berlin to Shanghai and down to what was once Saigon—in all of which there are neither free markets nor free men. For the U.S., 1776 and 1936 are the vintage years for ideas regarding how

---

*By strange coincidence Keynes was born in the year in which Marx died (1883), and on the same day, June 5, as Smith's birth is celebrated. (June 5 was really the date of his baptism; Smith's actual birthdate is not known.)

the state should behave in a world that includes both free markets and free people.

Events sometimes lead ideas, but more often the causality runs the other way round. On the final page of his enormously influential book, *The General Theory of Employment, Interest and Money* (whose publication is one reason 1936 is a watershed year), John Maynard Keynes, a fellow of King's College, Cambridge, wrote: "The ideas of economists and political philosophers, both when they are right and when they are wrong, are more powerful than is commonly understood. Indeed the world is ruled by little else. Practical men, who believe themselves to be quite exempt from any intellectual influences, are usually the slaves of some defunct economist. Madmen in authority, who hear voices in the air, are distilling their frenzy from some academic scribbler of a few years back."

No doubt Keynes was thinking of Adam Smith and Karl Marx when he wrote those words, but if we look at the opening sentence of the chapter in which the words appear, they also describe the influence his own book was to have for 40 years after it was published. The sentence reads: "The outstanding faults of the economic society in which we live are its failure to provide for full employment and its arbitrary and inequitable distribution of wealth and incomes." Decades later and thousands of miles to the west of Cambridge, England, U.S. policy devoted itself to correcting these two faults: Hundreds of statesmen, trained or inspired by scholars in Cambridge, Massachusetts, converted Keynes's 30-word statement into a torrent of legislation and regulation.

In order to understand the full import of the revolution in economic ideas that took place in 1936 and the constitutional revolution that occurred in the U.S. that same year, it is necessary to go back to two parallel revolutions that occurred in 1776 and that dominated political-economic thought and action for 150 years.

1776—Adam Smith

Two remarkable events occurred in 1776. One was the publication of Adam Smith's celebrated book, *The Wealth of Nations*. The other was the signing of the U.S. Declaration of Independence and the drafting of the Articles of Confederation, the forerunner of the Constitution.

Smith's great work rigorously established a then novel set of economic ideas:

1. It is not nature that produces wealth; people do.
2. The true wealth of nations does not lie in its stocks of gold or silver; it depends on aggregate supply, i.e., the total

annual output of goods and services that all the people of a nation produce and consume (what we now call the GNP).

3. Individuals who pursue their own best (selfish) interest in the marketplace will be guided "as if by an *invisible* hand" to maximize the overall best interest of society as a whole. In other words, through the forces of competition and rivalry between sellers and buyers, the pursuit of individual profit maximization leads to maximum economic welfare for society as a whole.

4. Government should, in the main, leave the determination of economic activity and rewards to the free working of the competitive marketplace.

Smith, although a proponent of a laissez-faire economy, did not suggest that there was no role for the government to play. There was an important, but confined, role for government. That role was to ensure competition in the marketplace and to provide "public goods and services," i.e., goods and services that only the government can provide in a society of free individuals—the common defense, law and order, such things as highways and other commonly used public facilities of the kind that no one person or company would or could finance because their services would or should be publicly available.

Smith's book was both the revolutionary manifesto and the rationale for the system of free-market capitalism that blossomed so well in the West after 1776. The ideas Smith expressed had an enormous impact on the world. As one German student put it in 1810, "Next to Napoleon, Adam Smith is now the mightiest monarch in Europe." As Smith predicted, even before the industrial age really began, a political-economic system of free markets and free individuals, who specialize in what each does best and who exchange the products of their work, did lead to impressive economic growth and progress for the society as a whole. Such growth was most impressive in the countries that adopted or seemed to adopt his ideas—notably in the United States where the role and share of the central government in economic affairs—i.e., the government call on national resources—was among the lowest in all the industrial world from 1776 to 1936.

Although the political-economic system practiced in the U.S. prior to 1936 appeared to fit the dictates of the Smithian model (even better than the system that was followed in the land of Smith's birth), it is not at all clear that this result was a simple consequence of the powerful ideas laid down in *The Wealth of Nations*. It is equally likely that the tiny economic role the federal government played in the economy prior to 1936 was the result of our Constitution and our tendency to rely on judicial interpretation of that document and legal procedures.

1776 and the U.S. Constitution

The Constitution of the United States was man's first and thus far most lasting attempt to define in writing the proper relationship between a government and the individuals by whose consent it governs. In defining the all-important relationship between government and the economy, a key phrase in the Constitution turned out to be the ambiguous phrase "to promote the general welfare." We do not know just whose pet phrase it was, but the "general welfare" appears in the Articles of Confederation and twice in the Constitution—first in the brief Preamble to the document and again in the opening paragraph of Section 8 of Article I in which the powers of the Congress to tax and spend are explicitly enumerated. Section 8 is one long sentence. It was obviously written by a committee because it runs to almost 500 words. In essence it says:

> Congress shall have the power to lay and collect taxes . . . to pay the debts and provide for the common defense and general welfare of the United States . . .
> To borrow money . . .
> To regulate Commerce . . .
> To coin money and regulate the value thereof and of foreign coin . . .
> To establish post offices and post roads . . .
> There follow a dozen other specific purposes starting with "to" and then finally these words: "To make all laws which shall be necessary and proper for carrying into execution the foregoing powers. . . ."

Was the phrase "to promote the general welfare" an explicit purpose for which the Congress was to have the power to raise taxes, spend money, and make laws? Or alternatively was it simply a qualifying phrase which governed the purposes that were later explicitly enumerated? This was no tiny semantic quibble, for on its outcome hung the history of what was to become the world's largest economy.

James Madison, who contributed the most to the actual writing of the Constitution, and Thomas Jefferson clearly interpreted "to promote the general welfare" in the narrow sense, as merely a qualifying phrase: Congress could pass laws, impose taxes, and spend money to carry out all of the *enumerated* purposes only *insofar* as these activities would contribute to the general welfare.

Others, notably Alexander Hamilton, argued that the phrase had much wider import: that the general welfare clause conferred a power separate and distinct from those later enumerated and therefore that the federal government could impose taxes and spend money for any purpose that would "promote the general welfare." In many ways Hamilton was the prototypical interventionist—an enormously brilliant man who believed that bright people, given the power to rule, could promote the welfare of all the people through strong government action.

The debate between the Madison-Jefferson wing of opinion and the Hamilton wing over the general welfare clause was part of a larger debate between them on the constitutional limits to the powers of the federal government. On some of the issues, Hamilton's views prevailed, notably with regard to his plan to establish a Bank of the United States. Jefferson objected to the proposed bank on the ground that there was no specific authorization for it in the Constitution. Hamilton's counterargument was that the power to establish such a bank was clearly "implied" in the specifically enumerated power "to collect taxes and regulate Commerce." Congress passed the bill establishing the bank and the bill was signed into law by President Washington in 1791. The doctrine of "implied" powers was later confirmed by Chief Justice Marshall in a major opinion in 1819.

Later in 1791 Hamilton presented his fourth and boldest report to Congress—the *Report on Manufactures.* Anticipating that his recommendation would be objected to on constitutional grounds, he specifically worked into it a defense based on his own constitutional interpretation of the general welfare clause:

> The National Legislature has express authority "to lay and collect taxes . . . and provide for the . . . general welfare. . . . These three qualifications excepted, the power to *raise money* is *plenary* and *indefinite.* . . . The phrase [general welfare] is as comprehensive as any that could have been used, because it was not fit that the constitutional authority of the Union to appropriate its revenues should have been restricted within narrower limits than the "general welfare," and because this necessarily embraces a vast variety of particulars, which are susceptible neither of specification nor of definition.
>
> It is, therefore, of necessity, left to the discretion of the National Legislature to pronounce upon the objects, which

concern the general welfare, and for which, under that description, an appropriation of money is requisite and proper.

As Hamilton expected, there was powerful opposition in the Congress, notably from Madison, who repeated his strongly held view that
the words general welfare were simply "a sort of caption or general
description of the specific powers" and gave "no further power" than
what could be "found in that specification." He continued: "I venture
to declare it as my opinion that were the power of Congress to be
established in the latitude contended for, it would subvert the very
foundation and transmute the very nature of the limited government
established by the people of America; and what inferences might be
drawn, or what consequences ensue from such a step, it is incumbent
on us all well to consider."*

Madison was convincing. Hamilton suffered a major defeat in the
House. His *Report on Manufactures* was pigeonholed. This outcome did
as much as Adam Smith's economic philosophy to keep the role and
share of the U.S. government in the economy confined to a very small
fraction for the next 140 years. Although various sorts of welfare legislation were passed, federal government expenditures "to promote the
general welfare" remained insignificant until the 1930s. Indeed in 1929
total federal spending (including defense expenditure) amounted only
to $2.6 billion—less than 2½ percent of the GNP in that year.

All this changed in 1936.

1936—The Keynesian Revolution

After 1929 the U.S. and other industrial nations fell into a deep and
prolonged economic recession. In the U.S., by 1933 the dollar value of
annual output (GNP) had fallen to one-half of its pre-1929 level; the rate
of unemployment had risen to 25 percent of the labor force; half of the
nation's banks had been closed, insolvent. The self-regulating market
economy posited by Adam Smith was no longer regulating itself: The
invisible hand had become all thumbs. Keynes's book, *The General Theory*, provided an explanation for what had happened: Smith's laissez-
faire, no-intervention economy worked well for part or most of the time;
it did not work *all* of the time. At particular times, such as the early
1930s, a lack of sufficient *aggregate demand* could cause supply activity
(output) to fall, and once that fall began there was no automatic mechanism to ensure that it would rise again. The *only* available cure for the
disease was for the government to intervene in order to stimulate ag-

* I am indebted to Mortimer J. Adler and William Gorman in *The American Testament* (New York, Praeger Publishers,
1975) pp. 102–103, for the quoted passages used above.

gregate demand artificially—either by increasing government spending (without raising taxes) or by cutting taxes (without reducing spending), i.e., by engineering a sizeable federal budget deficit.

As a result of Keynes's book the older idea that the government should balance its budget year in and year out was replaced by the idea that government should deliberately increase its spending or lower taxes and deliberately run a budget deficit in order to stimulate aggregate demand whenever a substantial part of the aggregate supply capacity of labor and capital was being left unused because of lack of demand from purely private forces. The use of fiscal policy to stimulate demand was given impeccable academic respectability by a scholar who was then the world's leading economic theorist.

As was true of Adam Smith, the revolutionary ideas that Keynes put forward in 1936 received worldwide acceptance but had their greatest impact in the United States. Once again it was not the revision in economic theory alone that brought about the dramatic change in the conduct of U.S. economic policies. It was political circumstance and a revised interpretation of the meaning of the "general welfare" clause in the Constitution.

The federal government did run budgetary deficits throughout the depression decade of the 1930s, but these deficits did not reflect the kind of expansionist fiscal policy Keynes had prescribed as a cure for insufficient aggregate demand. From 1931 to 1937, U.S. tax rates were raised year after year in order to minimize the deficit. Indeed President Franklin Roosevelt got elected in 1932 promising to balance the budget. This remained his obsession until at least 1938.

It was only after the huge increase in World War II related expenditures drove the U.S. economy rapidly to full employment that U.S. policy began to accept the theoretical prescription of Keynes's book. By then we had witnessed the beginning of a significant switch to a growing government role in the economy. As we will see shortly, this policy shift sprang primarily from a political rather than an economic rationale.

1936 and the U.S. Constitution

Driven by the pressing emergencies that were created by economic depression, the Roosevelt administration moved aggressively to assist large parts of the private sector. In agriculture, housing, social security, unemployment, and industry the government pushed forward a series of uncoordinated acts that were collectively called the "New Deal." These acts had one thing in common: Most went far beyond the congressional taxing, spending, and lawmaking powers enumerated in Section 8, Article I, of the Constitution as it had been interpreted by the Congress back in 1791. The legality of some of these acts was contested in the courts. Several of these contests reached the Supreme Court.

A key case, *United States* v. *Butler* (which involved the legality of using tax monies to pay farmers subsidies for *not* producing farm products), was decided in 1936. One relevant issue in the case turned out to be the scope and meaning of the "general welfare" clause in the Constitution: Did the government have the right to impose and use taxes for *any* purpose that in its belief would promote the "general welfare"? This was the old argument on which Hamilton (who thought it did) had lost to Madison and Jefferson a century and a half earlier. In 1936 the Court, in a decision written by Justice Roberts on the meaning of the "general welfare" clause, ruled that Hamilton's view was indeed the correct one: "The power of Congress to authorize expenditure of public monies for public purposes is not limited by the direct grants of legislative power found in the Constitution."

After that 1936 decision and several others that followed, the federal government could legally spend public funds for the purpose of "promoting the general welfare." The government proceeded to do so, cautiously at first and then after World War II at an accelerating rate.

The first exuberant expansion of the government's now fully constitutional "general welfare" powers took place in 1944 when President Roosevelt, turning from the conduct of war to the conduct of peace, presented Congress with an ambitious "Economic Bill of Rights" and challenged them to find means of implementing it.

In one sense the 1944 Bill of Rights was a U.S. response to the two indictments Keynes had levied in 1936: "The outstanding faults of the economic society in which we live are its failure to provide for full employment and its arbitrary and inequitable distribution of income." But Roosevelt's agenda went further. In addition to the right to a job and a decent income for all citizens, it included the right to decent housing, adequate medical care, a good education, and freedom from the economic fears of old age, sickness, accident, and unemployment.

By 1965 much of the ambitious agenda of 1944 had been achieved. The problem of supplying the ever-increasing flow of output required to meet those expansive economic goals for a growing population appeared to have been solved. As Norman Macrae, deputy editor of *The Economist*, expressed it, "The United States in this last third of the twentieth century is the place where man's long economic problem is ending, but where his social problems still gape" (*The Economist*, May 10, 1969). After 1965, the national agenda was enlarged to include a more definitive implementation of the goals enumerated by President Roosevelt 20 years earlier, and widened to include several new goals, the most notable of which was environmental protection. Progress toward the expanding agenda of objectives was achieved, but it was not achieved without cost. The steady shift of the nation's attention and resources toward some priorities, functions, and social groups necessarily diverted attention and resources away from others. The process was complex. It is easier to indicate the direction of the shifts that occurred as is done in the listing below than it is to classify or measure them in a regular table. The major shifts were as follows:

From	To
Supply	Demand
Savers	Borrowers
Private Sector	Public Sector
Workers	Nonworkers
The Young	The Old
Localities	States
States	Federal
Defense Spending	Nondefense Spending
Risk Takers	Bureaucrats
Investment	Consumption
Market Processes	Political Processes
Efficiency	Equality
Equality of Opportunity	Equality of Results
Growth of Income	Distribution of Income
Economy	Environment

Until 1965 the perceived costs of these collective shifts appeared to be small relative to the benefits. On the whole the programs were both emotionally appealing and economically successful. The key reason for the sense of success was that productivity expanded rapidly between 1948 and 1966. Real output available per worker (adjusted for both inflation and government's increasing share) rose by 53 percent between 1948 and 1966, a large rise that more than fully matched expectations. Between 1966 and 1973 the growth of productivity slowed markedly even as government's share in output kept on rising. Real output available per worker increased by only 4 percent in those seven years. After 1973 the situation worsened still further. Between 1973 and 1980 the gain in productivity per worker slowed to just 2.5 percent for the entire seven-year period, but government's share in output kept on rising. As a result real output available per worker fell by 1.5 percent between 1973 and 1980. By 1980, which was not a very good year, real output available per worker was falling at the rate of 3.2 percent *a year.*

In 1980 the fundamental pain of a falling reward for work was exacerbated by a number of other aches and irritations: a growing realization that the U.S. had permitted a significant decline in its military power; an annual inflation rate that had risen to a new record high of 13.5 percent; mortgage interest rates that had put home ownership beyond the reach of most workers who did not already own their homes; the legislated entitlement of larger (and unfixed) increases in income for nonworkers than for those who work.

By 1980 a majority of the people had shifted their support from the Keynes-Hamilton wing of opinion to the Smith-Madison position in the ongoing debate over the government's proper role in promoting "the general welfare."

The Size and Share of Government

Between 1965 and 1980 both the size and scope of the federal government were expanded rapidly. By mid-1981 the flow of U.S. output directly controlled by the government (including state and local units) exceeded one trillion dollars a year for the first time, an amount about equal to the total GNP of Japan. To put it more dramatically, if on June 30, 1981, President Mitterand of France had nationalized every single producer of goods and services in the French economy, the absolute size of France's socialized sector would have been only one-half the absolute size of the socialized sector of U.S. economic output! There is, of course, an important difference: In France, which tends to follow the more orthodox road to socialism, the government legally takes over the means of production; in the U.S. the government has left the means of production in private hands but has taken increasing control over the fruits of production.

Absolute comparisons of the kind made above are partly misleading because they ignore the total size of the U.S. economy. A better yardstick for the size and growth of government would be to look at its *share* in the U.S. economy, i.e., as the ratio of output allocated by the government to total available output. Measuring this ratio of the government's call on the nation's resources is not as straightforward as it might seem at first glance. The numerator of the ratio and the denominator can each be defined in three or four different ways, thus yielding ten or more answers to the question: Just how large is the government's share in the economy?

So far as the denominator is concerned, a common practice is to use the *gross national product* to measure the total economy. As the name implies, the GNP is the largest measure of the market value of society's total economic output. But all of this output is not freely available for use by either the private or the public sector. Part of this output has to be reinvested in order to maintain the preexisting stock of capital used in generating each year's output. If we deduct, set aside, and reinvest an appropriate amount each year to offset the annual depreciation of the nation's capital stock, what is left is known as the NNP, the *net national product*. NNP is a more accurate measure of the total output available for apportionment between private uses and uses that are essentially determined by the government.

At the other extreme from those who use the GNP to estimate government's share, some analysts use the smallest measure of national output. This measure, known as the *national income*, is an estimate of the total income earned by all the nation's factors of production (land, labor, and capital). The principal difference between the national income and the net national product is that the former excludes whereas the latter includes the annual value of indirect taxes (such as sales taxes) flowing to the government sector.

The differences between the three alternative measures of "total output" are quite large. During the first quarter of 1981, U.S. GNP was running at an annual rate of $2,853 billion;* the NNP was equal to $2,546 billion (89 percent of GNP); and the national income was $2,291 billion (80 percent of GNP). In what follows we will use the NNP.

There are equally large ambiguities on the numerator side of the ratio we seek to measure. Exactly how should the dollar amount of output used by the government be defined? There is an entire spectrum of concepts and numbers from which we can choose.

Taxes

Taxes paid to government give us one obvious measure of government's share in output. For many people the "cost of government" is simply the taxes they pay. During the first quarter of 1981 the federal government collected taxes at the rate of $621 billion per annum and state and local governments at $322 billion. The total share of taxes was thus $943 billion or 37 percent of the net national product. The composition of taxes in early 1981 is shown in Table 4.

The tax burden, i.e., taxes per dollar of NNP, has risen steadily since 1965 when it was just below 30 percent. The rate of rise accelerated over the five-year period from early 1976 to early 1981. One reason for the increase is that some tax *rates* were increased, notably Social Security taxes. A more important reason for the increased tax burden is that high

*This figure and others cited in this chapter are seasonally adjusted, annualized data from the official *U.S. National Income and Product Accounts*.

**Table 4: Composition of Federal, State, and Local Taxes
During the First Quarter of 1981**
(billions of dollars, seasonally adjusted annual rate)

	Federal	State and Local	Total
Personal Income Taxes	$277	$ 50	$327
Social Insurance Taxes	199	35	234
Corporate Income Taxes	78	13	91
Property Taxes	—	70	70
All other	67	154	221
Total	$621	$322	$943

rates of inflation in conjunction with our progressive personal income tax system pushed individuals into higher and higher tax brackets.

In the first quarter of 1976 total personal income taxes, then running $158 billion a year, took 14 percent of the total income earned by persons. Five years later, during the first quarter of 1981, personal income taxes had more than doubled to $327 billion a year and took 16½ percent of the total income earned by persons. This rise in the average tax rate took place even though there had been no legislated increase in tax rates. It was caused by what has come to be known as "bracket creep"— the process by which inflation pushes taxpayers into higher tax brackets on our progressive income tax scale.

What really matters for each taxpayer, so far as personal income taxes are concerned, is the additional tax that must be paid on an additional dollar of income—the ratio that economists refer to as the *marginal* tax rate. Between 1976 and 1981 total personal income rose by $841 billion. Well over two-thirds of the rise was attributable solely to inflation. However, our tax system does not recognize any difference between a genuine rise in income (which should be taxed) and a rise caused solely by inflation (which should not be taxed, but is). Additional taxes were payable on the entire additional $841 billion of income and the tax increase amounted to $170 billion: The marginal rate of taxation was therefore over 20 percent, compared to the basic rate of 14 percent paid in 1976.

The effect of bracket creep on a typical family, i.e., a taxpaying family of four which is just earning the median income earned by all families, is another useful way of looking at the same phenomenon. In 1965 the highest federal income tax bracket for the median family was 17 percent. If this median family increased its annual earnings by $1,000 it would have to pay an additional $170 in personal income taxes to the federal government. The corresponding marginal tax rate for a family earning *twice* the median was 22 percent. By 1981 the top federal bracket for the median family has risen from 17 percent to 28 percent. For a family earning twice the median the marginal tax rate had leaped from 22 percent to 43 percent. Again, all of this took place without a single congressman having to sign his name to a legislated increase in tax rates.

What is true of federal income taxes applied equally to state and local income taxes. In California, for example, the maximum tax rate of 11 percent on additional income is reached whenever an individual earns more than just $16,000 a year. For the median family in California the combined federal and state income tax and Social Security taxes payable on $100 of additional earnings was approximately 40 percent in 1981, a tax burden once intended only for the very rich.

Spending

Taxes measure the government's share in the economy only if government spending is equal to or less than the taxes it raises. But what if expenditures exceed taxes, as has been the situation for the federal government throughout the decade of the 1970s? When expenditures exceed taxes, the level of federal spending is a more accurate measure of the share of economic resources over which the government exercises command. By this measure—federal spending (plus state and local taxes)—government was "using" $995 billion or 39 percent of our net national production during the second quarter of 1981. Federal spending alone was equal to 26.1 percent of the NNP during this period.

The figures given above refer to federal expenditures that are presented in the official U.S. budget. However, this statistic excludes two significant off-budget items that should (arguably) be included. The first item consists of receipts such as those arising from the leasing of federal lands for mineral development. These receipts are not counted as "revenues" in the official federal budget. They are treated as an "offset" to total federal expenditures, thus reducing official expenditures. The second and larger item consists of borrowing by special federal agencies (such borrowing is not included in the official deficit) for the purpose of financing subsidized mortgages or loans to specific areas or groups in society.

Just how these items affect the "true" share of government's control over the allocation of the national product is a controversial matter. A large number of economists, perhaps the majority, would include both items in the annual amount of resources that the government controls. If we add these to our numerator, government's total take from the economy was running at an annual rate of $1,040 billion during the second quarter of 1981, or at 41 percent of the net national product.

Compliance Costs

The conclusion that government's share in the economy was around 40 percent in mid-1981 does not include the private cost of complying with the rising volume of regulations imposed by the government. Should it do so? For many observers the answer is a clear yes. Their logic is simple. Assume that the pharaoh of Egypt proclaims that there will be no taxes payable to the state but that every ablebodied person must spend one day a week to help the state build a pyramid. What is the government's share of national output? Obviously it is one-seventh or about 14 percent. In economic terms, the cost of compulsory compliance with a governmental edict amounts to the same thing as a tax. Conceptually, such costs should be counted in government's share. The problem is to find a good statistical estimate of compliance costs. Collectively, we install or buy mandated antipollution or safety equipment devices, fill out tax forms, maintain records, respond to departmental questionnaires, file environmental impact studies, and do a hundred other things because the law requires us to do so.

A torrent of legislation in the 1960s and 1970s regarding environmental protection, worker health and safety, and equal opportunity had led to a large increase in compliance costs which only the bravest statisticians and accountants have tried to measure. Their estimates for total compliance costs in early 1981 range around $140 billion or just over 5 percent of the net national product. Including these admittedly crude estimates, government—federal, state, and local—was using or directing the uses of 46 percent of the total available flow of U.S. economic output in 1981!

Size and Growth

Debating the exact size and share of the government in the economy is interesting mainly to technicians. The range of possible answers to the share question is somewhere between 22 and 52 percent. If we pick the smallest possible numerator (just federal taxes) and the largest possible denominator (GNP), we can say that government's share in the economy in early 1981 was *only* 22 percent. If we pick the largest possible numerator (federal spending and lending *plus* state and local taxes *plus* the private cost of complying with regulations) and the smallest possible denominator (the national income), we can say that government's share was over 50 percent.

The related question of how fast government's share in the economy

"Squeeze Play"

Drawing by Art Wood
Courtesy *Farm Bureau News*

has grown allows even more leeway for nimble statistical footwork. In addition to selecting the yardstick to be used, it allows one to select the period over which comparisons are made in order to present the best case for whatever argument one is making.

For example, to demolish the widely held perception of rapid federal government growth during the 1970s, one can cite the fact that federal civilian employment in 1979 (2.77 million) was no higher than it had been in 1969 (2.77 million). The statement is true but not really meaningful. The federal government's share in the economy can be increased in many ways without adding a single person to the regular federal payroll:

1. The federal government can finance the growth of state and local government employment. Between 1970 and 1980 federal grants-in-aid to state and local governments quadrupled (from $22 billion to $87 billion). During the same period government employment at the state and local levels rose from 9.8 million to 13.3 million, a rise of 36 percent against a population increase of under 9 percent.

2. The federal government can hire firms and individuals in the private sector to do government's work under contract. The volume of such contracting also increased rapidly during the 1970s.

3. The federal government can require or induce the private sector to hire employees or retain consultants whose principal intended task is to ensure compliance with laws and regulations issued by the government. There are no hard estimates of the exact fraction of private sector employment that is essentially devoted to "public" functions, but there is considerable evidence that this fraction grew rapidly in the 1970s. Thus, although direct federal employment itself did not grow at all in the 1970s, indirect employment grew rapidly enough to make Washington, D.C., one of the nation's fastest-growing large metropolitan areas in that decade.

4. The fourth and most important way in which the federal government's share can and did grow without any rise in direct employment is through a rise in the flow of governmental transfers of income from one sector of the economy to another.* Beginning with the Great Society programs enacted in 1964, the volume of such transfers (sometimes referred to as entitlement programs) rose extremely rapidly. Between 1964 and 1980 there occurred a tenfold increase in the annual flow of federally financed transfers to individuals, well over twice the corresponding increase in the national output of goods and services.

---

*A transfer payment is defined as any payment (in cash or kind) which does not represent a reward for economic services currently rendered.

The Election of 1980

The important issue in the election of 1980 was not the exact share of government in the economy or the exact rate at which that share had grown. By even the simplest of obvious measures, i.e., total taxes as a share of the GNP, the government's share was very much larger in 1980 (33 percent) than it had been in 1929 (10 percent). The debate in 1980 was about two deeper issues:

1. Was the government's enlarged intervention in the economy providing aggregate benefits to society that were larger than their aggregate costs?
2. Should government's rising share in the economy continue to be increased in the 1980s?

Before 1965 the public's answer to both questions was affirmative. After 1965 the answers to both questions began to drift into the opposite column. By 1980 the consensus on both had turned to "No." In what might eventually turn out to be a watershed election, the voters in 1980 selected a new government unambiguously committed to the goal of reversing the trend of rising public intervention that had been in process for almost 50 years.

"YOU MEAN THERE'S A LIMIT TO HOW MANY WISHES I GET?"

Drawing by Herblock
© 1981 Herblock in *The Washington Post*

6

Beyond the Turning Point

IN 1981 THE U.S. WITNESSED what could well turn out to be another major historic turning point in the long-run thrust of its economic policies. When President Reagan took office in January of that year, he was already openly committed to reversing the directions along which the nation's policies had been moving for decades. Within seven months of his inauguration, his administration had put into effect a comprehensive set of policy shifts bold enough to start the reversal he sought. The new policies had five major components:

1. *Tax Cuts.* The largest component of the 1981 reform was the enactment of sharp cuts in federal tax rates on individual incomes, business incomes, gifts, and estates. Taken together, these reductions amounted to the largest single tax cut in the nation's history. The four principal cuts were: a 23 percent reduction in individual income tax rates to take place in three steps over a 33-month period; an immediate cut (effective January 1982) from 70 percent to 50 percent in the "penalty" maximum tax rate previously applicable to unearned income (income from interest and dividends); a reduction from 28 percent to 20 percent in the maximum tax rate on long-term capital gains; finally, a significant liberalization of the rates at which capital assets could be depreciated for business tax accounting purposes.

2. *Spending Cuts.* The second component of the reform was a large

cutback in the future rise of federal expenditures. The spending budget for fiscal year 1982 was reduced by about $40 billion relative to the budget that outgoing President Carter had presented to the Congress just a few months earlier. Most but not all of the cutbacks required and received legislative approval.

In spite of the cutback in total federal spending, spending for national defense was increased, with further large increases scheduled for the 1983–86 period. In the early 1960s, before the Vietnam War, the U.S. had allocated about 9 percent of its annual GNP to defense. After Vietnam, the share of defense in the budget was reduced rapidly; by 1980 it was down to just over 5 percent of GNP. Under the Reagan budget proposals, the share of defense spending was scheduled to rise to 7 percent of annual GNP by 1984, a schedule that implied a real rise of 7 percent a year in defense outlays.

3. *Budget Balance by 1984.* The third item in the Reagan program was a commitment to balance the federal budget by fiscal year 1984. In spite of rapidly rising taxes, federal spending had exceeded federal revenues by large amounts in every single year for over a decade. As a result, from fiscal 1970 to fiscal 1981 the national debt had grown from $370 billion to $1,000 billion.

4. *Regulatory Abatement.* The fourth item in the program was an undertaking to reduce and keep on reducing rising burdens that federal regulations had imposed on the private economy. Unnecessary regulations and unnecessary cabinet-level departments such as Energy and Education were to be dismantled.

5. *Monetary Discipline.* The fifth item was a promise to allow and encourage the Federal Reserve System to conduct policies that would result in a steady and predictable decline in the growth rate of the nation's money supply stringent enough to reduce the rate of inflation to 5 percent a year by 1984.

The ultimate purpose of the Reagan economic program was to reverse two basic adverse developments that had taken place between 1965 and 1980—a large and steady rise in the rate of inflation from 1½ percent prior to 1965 to 13½ percent in 1980, and a large and steady fall in the rate of productivity gain from the 3 percent level of 1965 to below zero by 1980. The success or failure of the 1981 turn in policy will depend on how well it spurs the economy on to improved performance on both of these fronts. What follows discusses three aspects of the relationship between the Reagan economic program and its ultimate objectives:

1. What was the program's underlying rationale?

2. Why was the initial reaction of the marketplace, especially that of the financial markets, so negative?
3. What are the chances that the turn in policy will in fact achieve the desired turn in economic performance?

The Reagan Economic Program

The Reagan administration chose not to pin a label on its overall economic program. The program nonetheless attracted several descriptive labels from the press, among them: supply-side economics, monetarism, neoconservatism, free-market economics, and, predictably, Reaganomics. All of them fit partly but none (except the last) fits exactly. The reason is simple. The individual labels do not refer to precisely defined concepts; a mixture of them, such as the Reagan program was, is therefore even less precisely definable in terms of any single label. To confuse the issue, the labels are not mutually exclusive—most Republican economists belong to all four schools of thought.

Supply-Side Economics

The idea of a supply-side approach to economic policy is not really a new one. Indeed most of the principal ideas in Adam Smith's great work were essentially supply-side ideas—the efficiency of the division of labor, the productivity of free trade and free markets, the necessity for the accumulation of capital, the counterproductive effects of certain types of taxes and governmental interventions.

The Keynesian revolution of the 1930s asserted that in a modern economy demand rather than supply is the principal determinant of national employment and output. Thereafter the main emphasis of policy increasingly shifted to the demand side of the equation—to the use of fiscal, monetary, and other policies for the purpose of creating and maintaining full employment and providing for a more equitable distribution of income and other social objectives. The effects of these policies on the supply side of the national economic equation came gradually to be ignored.

The adverse economic developments of the 1970s—the deterioration in the rate of productivity improvement and worsening inflation—discredited the by-then-almost-exclusive attention of neo-Keynesian economics on short-run demand management and led to a lively revival of attention to the supply side. Thus, what is now called supply-side economics was reborn—classical economics in modern dress. The general conclusion of those who now label themselves supply-side economists was that by the 1970s the accumulated weight of U.S. economic policies on taxation, spending, money creation, and regulation had become a major drag on U.S. productivity performance. This conclusion and the policy prescriptions to which it pointed provided one important basis for the Reagan economic program. It shaped the size and form of the 1981 tax and budget cuts and accounted for the emphasis the program placed on reducing those regulatory burdens that inhibited productive economic activity.

The logic of supply-side thinking and its contrast to what might be labeled neo-Keynesian demand-side thinking is best illustrated by the fundamental differences between the Reagan tax cut of 1981 and the tax cut Congress enacted during the Ford administration in 1975. In summary, the differences were as follows:

The specific purpose of the 1975 tax cut was to provide a temporary stimulus to demand in order to offset a recession, but without any serious long-run revenue loss to the government. A secondary purpose was to redistribute income to lower income groups. By contrast the purpose of the 1981 tax cut was to increase incentives to produce by increasing net rewards available to individuals on increases in the income they could earn in the future. Furthermore the cut in tax rates was meant to be permanent, and no attempt was made to use the tax system to redistribute income upward or downward.

The form of the two tax cuts clearly reflected their different purposes. The main provision of the 1975 act was a rebate to taxpayers of 10 percent of their 1974 income taxes, subject to a maximum rebate of $200 per taxpayer regardless of actual 1974 taxes, and to a minimum rebate of $100. For 1975, income taxes payable were also reduced through a $30 tax credit per taxpayer and dependent, the introduction of a "negative" tax for low-income taxpayers, and an increase in the standard deduction allowed each taxpayer—methods designed to provide higher relative reductions to individuals earning lower incomes. By contrast the 1981 tax act provided virtually equal across-the-board cuts in all tax rates.

A third difference lay in the expectation (and hope) that taxpayers would spend their increase in disposable income in 1975 whereas in 1981 the expectation (and hope) was that a significant portion of increased disposable income would be saved and invested.

Monetarism

A monetarist is someone who believes in two sets of propositions: first, that an excessive rise in the total supply of money is the critical force that causes a rise in the general price level, and hence who believes that proper control over the growth in the supply of money is the single

"I'm an Episcopalian on my mother's side and a
supply-sider on my father's."

critical element in reducing the rate of inflation; second, that the proper purpose to which national monetary control should be directed is the stability of the general price level. In the short run, actions to control the money supply may and frequently do have significant effects on a nation's interest rates and on exchange rates. In the monetarist view, monetary policy should give little or no weight to those short-run considerations. Rather it should devote itself single-mindedly to its legitimate objective of achieving price stability. In the long run, reducing inflation also will bring about an enduring reduction in interest rates as well as exchange-rate stability relative to other noninflationary currencies.

Although several postwar administrations had subscribed in principle to these views, few (with the notable exception of the Eisenhower administration) had been willing to tolerate the consistent use of a monetarist policy in practice. The Reagan program contained an explicit commitment to monetarism, i.e., to a policy of reducing and stabilizing the growth of the money supply in order to bring about a steady reduction in the rate of inflation to 5 percent by 1984. In that sense the program had monetarist roots.

Neoconservatism

Like supply-side economics, neoconservatism with regard to economic policy is a classical tradition going back to Presidents Madison and Lincoln: the tradition that the federal government's role in the economy essentially should be concentrated on doing things that only the federal government can do—ensure the national defense, regulate the value of money, provide for law and order. The list of the federal government's functions has obviously expanded over the decades. The thrust of neoconservatism is to hold future extension of the government's role to essentials and to suspend, eliminate, revise, or roll back inessential bureaucratic regulation. This philosophy represented another root of the Reagan economic program.

Free-Market Economics

A fourth source of ideas for the Reagan economic program was the belief that whenever one is feasible, a market solution is superior to a solution imposed on the economy by the government. Thus, the program rejected the idea that inflation should be controlled either through soft or hard federal government controls over specific wages, prices, credit, or exchange rates. By contrast many Keynesian economists had come to believe by 1980 that the marketplace, left to itself, was no longer capable of bringing about an orderly and enduring reduction in the rate of inflation.

Reaganomics

Like fashions in economic theory, fashions in labeling economic programs change. It used to be customary to use names like New Deal, Fair Deal, and Great Society to caption programs. These have been replaced by less imaginative words such as Nixonomics, Carternomics, and Reaganomics. The recent practice may be stylistically unaesthetic, but it does recognize that any new president's program is a unique mix, personally selected from a bewildering range of possible options. Although the Reagan program was an integrated attack on the problems which the U.S. economy faced in the 1980s, it did not coincide on all points with the preferred policy prescriptions of any particular group or subgroup of the many economists and advisers on whom the president drew from inside and outside the administration.

After the Reagan program's installation as a completed package—the large tax bill was finally enacted in early August 1981—differences between the many groups that had contributed to the program began to surface. These differences became sharper when the program itself appeared to run into difficulties shortly after the president won his incredible legislative victory on the tax bill.

Financial Market Reactions

Reaction in some circles to the Reagan program predictably was negative. The cutback in federal nondefense spending relative to what these expenditures might otherwise have run in fiscal 1982 amounted to $40 billion—a sum larger than the total annual flow of dividends paid by all U.S. corporations from their domestic operations in 1980! Both those who might have received that vast annual sum from society and those who would have dispensed it were distressed about its curtailment.

What was less predictable was the palpably negative response of U.S. financial markets. Between April and September 1981, interest rates, which previously had begun to fall, rose again to record or near-record levels: The prime rate charged by banks to their most credit-worthy borrowers rose from 17 percent to 20½ percent and remained there all summer; short-term rates rose from the 13 percent level to 18 percent; and the rising yields payable on long-term bonds and mortgages broke all previous records. The market values of bonds and mortgages, which move inversely with interest rates, fell sharply, causing severe losses to individuals and financial institutions. By the end of the summer, stock prices, which joined the bearish parade in June, had on average fallen by 15 percent in less than three months.

In all, holders of bonds, mortgages, and common stocks suffered losses in the market value of assets that added up to a half a trillion dollars. It was not an auspicious beginning for a program that had been enacted but was not even scheduled to go into effect until October 1, the start of the new fiscal year.

Real Interest Rates

The losses suffered by holders of financial assets were serious, but a more serious problem during the summer of 1981 was the fact that interest rates had risen in spite of a significant decline in the inflation rate. As a result, the difference between the two rates (the rate of interest and the rate of inflation), sometimes referred to as the *real* rate of interest, rose to an extremely high level.

For the business sector of the economy, the level of the *real* rate is what actually matters. A farmer, a builder, a manufacturer, a wholesaler, or retailer can operate profitably in a world of 20 percent interest rates if prices are also rising at around 20 percent: The price increase provides the wherewithal to pay financing costs. By contrast a world of 20 percent interest rates in which prices are rising at well below 10 percent—the situation in the U.S. in the spring and summer of 1981—threatens the very survival of most small businesses. (Between March 1981 and August 1981 the Producer Price Index, the relevant price index for most businesses, rose at a rate of under 6 percent a year. The average prime rate during this period was nearly 20 percent.) One congressman on returning to Washington after the August 1981 recess described the nation's leading economic concern colorfully: "My constituents have just three concerns—interest rates, interest rates, and interest rates." Had he been an economist he might have said: "If the *real* rate of interest remains at the present level much longer, the majority of businesses in my constituency will soon be bankrupt."

The extraordinary level of real rates of interest which prevailed in the U.S. throughout most of 1981 caused as much pain outside the country as it did within. It was one factor that attracted funds from other currencies to the dollar and thus drove up the dollar's exchange rate. For example, between August 1980 and August 1981 the value of the U.S. dollar rose by 40 percent against the deutsche mark.

Because the price of oil is denominated in dollars, there was a corresponding rise in the German price of oil imports. In order to counter the rising dollar, West Germany had to take steps to increase her own interest rates toward the level prevailing in the U.S. even though her recessed economic conditions called for lower rather than higher interest rates. Chancellor Helmut Schmidt expressed his frustration to President Reagan at the 1981 Summit meetings in Canada by telling him that real interest rates had reached the highest level recorded since the birth of Christ! The chancellor may have been overstating a little but he was not far wrong. With the exception of periods in which the absolute level of prices is actually falling, the gap that emerged in the U.S. in 1981 between the level of interest rates and the rate of inflation was the largest experienced in this century. When he made his statement in May 1981, Chancellor Schmidt was pleading with President Reagan to take steps to reduce that gap and bring down interest rates. By September 1981 almost everybody else was pleading for the same outcome.

The Pressure on Interest Rates

Why was the real rate of interest as high as it was in the summer of 1981? In other words, why had nominal interest rates risen and stayed high even as the inflation rate was moving down? The phenomenon was clearly an aberration: For the preceding 20 years, inflation rates and interest rates had moved up and down in tandem so that the gap between the two was never large for long. During the first eight months of 1981 a gap of nearly 10 percentage points developed between the market rate of interest on short-term certificates of deposit (which remained high) and the rate of inflation as measured by the Producer Price Index (which fell steadily from January to August). History suggests that the aberrant gap would have to narrow sooner or later. The only question by September 1981 was how this narrowing would take place—through a renewed rise in inflation, through a fall in nominal interest rates, or through some combination of the two. There was no consensus on the issue, but a strong body of opinion on Wall Street predicted that both inflation and interest rates were destined to go much higher in 1982. The argument behind the prediction was that the Reagan policies did not "add up"—that there were serious inconsistencies among its several components.

One major inconsistency was the clash between the program's revenue and spending plans on the one hand and its commitment to reducing the size of the budget deficit to zero by fiscal 1984 on the other. Specifically, the Reagan plan projected the deficit coming down from an estimated $58 billion in fiscal 1981 to $42.5 billion in fiscal 1982, to $22 billion in fiscal 1983, and then to zero in fiscal 1984. However, such an outcome appeared to be quite unlikely: On the basis of tax cuts and budget cuts actually achieved, the prospective budget deficits for 1982–84 looked much larger than those outlined in the Reagan plan. When the tax act was approved, the prospective loss of revenue over the three-year period 1982–84 was estimated to be around $288 billion—about $40 billion in fiscal 1982, $100 billion in fiscal 1983, and $148 billion in fiscal 1984. On the spending side, Congress had approved spending cuts of $169 billion over the same three-year period, or about $119 billion less than the tax cut. Just to keep the size of the annual deficit down to its 1981 level of $58 billion from 1982 to 1984, the president would have to come up with another $119 billion in budget cuts over the three years. To balance the budget by 1984, he would have to come up with even more. Given these realities, the conclusion on Wall Street was that budget balance by 1984 could not be achieved. The likely prospect was a continuation of very high levels of deficit spending, not only in 1982 but in 1983 and 1984 as well. It was this prospect that kept interest rates abnormally high.

The Reagan program's inherent inconsistency can also be explained as follows: The thrust of fiscal policy over the period 1982–84 was going to be highly expansionary because of large increases in defense spending, large cuts in taxes, and large overall deficits. At the same time, the program planned to keep a firm throttle on the rate of growth in the supply of money and credit. The push of a loose fiscal policy grating against a regimen of tight monetary control would inevitably produce constant upward pressure on interest rates. On the other hand, if monetary policy was loosened in order to accommodate the expansive fiscal policy, inflation would worsen again, which in turn would cause interest rates to rise. For the bond market bears of Wall Street, the outlook was for more of the same trend that had savaged them so badly in the past— generally rising interest rates and falling bond prices interrupted only by brief reversals.

Deficits and Interest Rates

The Reagan administration was clearly disappointed by the negative reaction in the financial markets. The question is why the administration had not seen it coming.

One answer lies in the monetarist component of the program's basic design. For many monetarists there is no necessary connection between deficits and interest rates. Before we examine the basis of this conclusion, let us look at a second and altogether different explanation for why the Reagan program as initially installed was internally inconsistent. This alternative explanation is that a critical element was left out— that missing element was gold, i.e., a return to the gold standard and convertibility of the dollar into gold.

The Missing Element

One subgroup of supply-siders who participated in the formulation of the Reagan program—for want of a better descriptive name I will refer to them as the gold branch—believed that the principal reason for the very high level of U.S. interest rates was a lack of faith in the dollar, which in turn stemmed from a lack of faith in the ability of the monetary authorities to control inflation effectively. For them the only way for the U.S. to achieve *both* fast growth and a lasting reduction in inflation and interest rates required both a significant cut in taxes rates *and* a return to the gold standard. The Reagan program as it was enacted contained the first element but not the second. For them that was the main reason the program encountered difficulties in 1981. Furthermore, they felt the program would keep encountering difficulties unless the missing element was restored to it.

Although the gold-branch supply-siders seem to be pitted against the monetarist branch on the particular issue of replacing the existing system of monetary control with a gold standard, their thinking is highly monetarist in flavor and ascribes great weight to the critical role that money plays in the economy. Indeed, some of their ideas have been referred to as "global monetarism." What then is their quarrel with conventional monetarism? It is as follows: The critical operating variable for conventional monetary control over inflation is the *supply* of money and its rate of growth. For the gold branch such a policy of money-supply control had not succeeded in controlling inflation since the suspension of the dollar's convertibility into gold in 1971.* Nor could it succeed in 1981: Tight money could reduce the rate of inflation temporarily by inducing an economic recession, but the rate would rise again, probably to even higher levels, as soon as normal economic conditions were restored. Therefore, in their view, conventional monetarism could not provide a program that offered *both high growth and low inflation*, which is what the Reagan program is all about.

Their solution to the dilemma is to switch the emphasis from suppressing the supply of money to increasing the public's willingness to hold dollars and other financial instruments, such as bonds, that are denominated in dollars. The restoration of convertibility of the dollar into gold at a fixed rate is the method they advocate for bringing about that increase. Their argument is that soon after convertibility is announced, the public's confidence in holding dollars will rise and this would make possible a rapid expansion of the economy, indeed that inflation would subside and with it interest rates.

Whether or not the wave of a golden wand can transform a slow-growth, high-inflation economy into a fast-growth, low-inflation one is

*Until August 1971 dollars held by other central banks were theoretically freely convertible into gold. This privilege did not extend to others. In fact U.S. citizens were not free to own gold, except for ornamental purposes.

something we will not know for a while. There are formidable mechanical questions that have to be explored before convertibility could be restored, not the least of which is the thorny question of just where the price of gold should be set when full convertibility began again. A congressionally sponsored Gold Commission has been appointed to study the entire matter; its report is scheduled for presentation in 1982.

The Monetarist View

The monetarist view that there is no necessary connection between federal deficits and interest rates is based partly on theory and partly on observation of empirical data. So far as theory is concerned, monetarists believe that a rise in nominal interest rates is primarily caused by a rise in the expected inflation rate—that, by and large, real rates do not change much over short spans of time. Deficits can affect the rate of inflation but only if they are monetized, i.e., financed by the Federal Reserve System. If a deficit is not directly or indirectly financed by the Federal Reserve System, the deficit as such cannot raise the rate of inflation and hence will have no effect on interest rates.

Two kinds of empirical evidence have been cited to support the conclusion outlined. One is the historical observation that, in general, periods of falling interest rates have been associated with rising federal deficits. The second is to look at countries, such as Japan, which recently have been running deficits that are much larger than ours but which nonetheless enjoy much lower inflation and interest rates than we have experienced. Year after year Japan has financed around 30 percent of her total budget through borrowed funds: For example, in her 1980 fiscal year (from April 1, 1980, to March 31, 1981) the ratio of the deficit to total government expenditures was 33 percent and the ratio of the deficit to her GNP was nearly 6 percent. The corresponding U.S. figures (for calendar year 1980) were 10 percent and 2.3 percent. Yet during 1980 Japan had a much lower inflation rate than did the U.S. (7.0 percent versus our 12.5 percent) and much lower interest rates as well.

These observations are correct but they are also misleading. Let us take them in reverse order. The relevant ratio for judging the impact of a deficit is the ratio of the annual deficit to the annual flow of net saving available in the credit market, of which the largest component is personal saving. In Japan, households save at a far higher rate than is true in the U.S.; their ratio of personal saving to their GNP is around 15 percent, ours just below 4 percent. Their deficit in 1980 was nearly 6 percent of their GNP, but financing it absorbed less than 40 percent of total available personal saving; our deficit was "only" 2.3 percent of GNP, but it absorbed nearly 60 percent of total available personal saving.

In that sense our deficit exerted greater pressure on interest rates in the financial markets.

It is also true that we have seen interest rates fall even as deficits rise, but this has occurred only during periods of recession. Rising deficits during nonrecession periods generally have been associated with rising interests rates. The reason is simple: Even if they are not monetized, deficits have to be financed by government borrowing in the market-place; if private demand for credit is also high, the competition for funds generates upward pressure on interest rates. This is precisely what the U.S. witnessed in 1981. What follows explains how and why.

During the first quarter of 1980 the economy was in an expansive phase; real output was rising and inflation was accelerating. As a consequence, private borrowing demand was high. In that quarter, the total volume of funds borrowed in all credit markets ran at an annualized rate of $403 billion, or 15.7 percent of GNP; of this the federal government borrowed the equivalent of 2.4 percent of GNP and the private sector borrowed the remaining 13.3 percent. Interest rates rose sharply during the quarter.

One quarter later, the economy fell into a deep but brief recession. Private borrowing demand also fell sharply: That is what a recession is all about. Consumers reduce their rate of new borrowing even as they pay off old debts; the volume of new mortgage lending falls; businesses liquidate inventories and repay their bank loans. In the aggregate, net private demand for funds fell from 13.3 percent of GNP to 7.2 percent. Government borrowing rose sharply—from a rate of $61 billion a year (2.4 percent of GNP) to $72 billion a year (2.8 percent of GNP), a very large rise for one quarter. Nonetheless interest rates *fell*, some short-term rates by nearly 50 percent. The reason for that sharp fall was that *total* borrowing demand (private plus government) had fallen sharply from 15.7 percent of GNP to just 10.0 percent of GNP.

After mid-1980 the economy recovered and the volume of private borrowing rose once more; by the first half of 1981 it had climbed to 11.5 percent of GNP. According to all the rules of an intelligent fiscal policy, the government's deficit and hence its need for funds should have fallen. But those rules had been annulled by extravagant and built-in budget increases. The government's deficit and hence its need for borrowed funds kept on rising, from 2.8 percent of GNP to 3.1 percent. The combined pressure of private and public borrowing demands now equal to nearly 15 percent of GNP drove interest rates up again to record or near-record levels. Thus in 1981, although the financial markets approved of what the Reagan economic policies had done to cut back both spending and tax rates, they feared the effects that continuously rising deficits would have on future interest rates. Just one example will show why these fears were not entirely irrational. Some of New York's most trusted trustees had invested their client's funds in what they once thought were safe, secure 8½ percent U.S. government bonds. They had purchased these bonds at par in 1974. By September 1981 rising interest rates had driven the market price of the bonds from $100 down to $60. On top of this disaster, inflation had reduced the value of the now $60 bond to just $33 in terms of the 1974 dollars they had paid when the bonds were purchased! Their not unfounded fear of seemingly uncontrollable deficits in the future kept them from purchasing more bonds during the summer of 1981. Thus those who needed to borrow funds, including the government itself, had to offer higher and higher rates of interest in order to induce the reluctant lenders to lend. The persistence of high interest rates forced the administration to restore credibility to its promise that the budget deficit was not out of control and that the budget would be balanced by 1984.

The Administration's Response

The spread of economic distress caused by the burden of record real rates of interest was not the only factor that forced a response from the administration in September 1981. By then there were widespread expectations that the deficit for fiscal 1982 was going to be far larger than the $42.5 billion estimate projected in July. Revised estimates showed that spending in fiscal 1982 was going to be at least $17.5 billion higher than had been planned. Unless new budget initiatives were introduced, the deficit would rise from $42.5 billion to $60 billion or more.

There was not much room for maneuver. The president had only four choices:

1. He could cut or defer defense spending.
2. He could raise new taxes or defer the cuts that had just been made.
3. He could ask for further cuts in nondefense spending. The problem here was that with Social Security virtually untouchable and interest payments absolutely so, he would have to ask for more saving from the programs that had already been cut back.
4. He could bow to the reality of a larger budget deficit than the $58 billion deficit for 1981 for which he had criticized the previous administration.

The president picked a combination of all four: a $2 billion cut in defense, an $11 billion cut in nondefense spending, a $3 billion increase through new tax and user fees, a reestimate that existing tax laws would generate $1 billion more than earlier estimated, and finally, a small increase in the deficit to $43 billion.

"There's no cause for panic, Mrs. Munson, but, frankly, there are certain indicators that cannot be ignored."

The package did little to calm a nervous market; it was too small and furthermore there was little assurance that Congress would grant the president the budgetary changes he sought. Given his four long-run commitments to strengthen defense, reduce taxes, implement tight monetary control, and cut back government intervention in the marketplace, there was not much else the president could do to alleviate the short-run problem presented by record high real rates of interest.

The Response of the Economy

So far as the economy itself was concerned, the problem of an extraordinary real rate of interest had to reach an early resolution in one way or another. If the government's net demand for funds could not be curbed in the short run either through a tighter budget or an easier monetary policy, there was only one alternative left: Private demand for funds had to fall. The only way this could come about was through a recession. By September 1981 it had become clear that a swing into another recession had become inevitable.

The U.S. Economy in the 1980s

In one sense the recession that began in 1981 was another, possibly final, phase in the process of the economy's adaptation to the vast imbalances that first became manifest in the early 1970s: the imbalance between the growth of the money supply and the growth of real output, the imbalance between the growth of energy demand and energy supply, and finally the imbalance between the growth of government and the growth of the private sector. The adaptation of policy toward resolving even some of these imbalances did not begin in earnest until the late 1970s. However by 1981, with the passage of the Reagan program, decisive steps had been taken to face up to, and correct, all three.

Will the turn in policies lead the economy and the financial markets to better performance in the future than they enjoyed in the past decade? Although it is too early to tell what the eventual outcome for the economy will be, there are grounds for optimism on at least one important front. In 1980 the U.S. dollar had suffered a continuation of its painful slide against most other yardsticks of value—gold, silver, oil, Swiss francs, and deutsche marks. In 1981 this slide was not only stopped; it was reversed.

1. In early 1980 the dollar price of gold had risen to $850 an ounce. By September 1981 the price of gold had fallen to just half that level. Silver suffered an even larger setback, from a peak price of nearly $50 an ounce to below $10 an ounce.

2. In 1980, the dollar price of petroleum, already very high, rose rap-

idly. Several oil-exporting countries were demanding and receiving over $40 a barrel. That rise also was reversed: By the late summer of 1981 the price of oil had actually begun to fall.

3. By July 1980 the dollar had fallen to 1.75 deutsche marks and 1.60 Swiss francs. This slide too was reversed: By July 1981, the dollar had risen by about 40 percent against these two key currencies.

In 1980 anybody who was prepared to forecast that the price of gold was headed for $2,000 an ounce or that oil was soon going to $100 a barrel or that the U.S. dollar would shortly be worth one Swiss franc had little trouble finding a paying audience. By September 1981 the audience had dwindled. The flight out of the dollar had been reversed. The cost to society of achieving that reversal was a record high level of interest rates.

As is true of most recessions, the recession that began in 1981 will have several predictable results. The rate of inflation and the level of interest rates will both fall. However there will be a cost to be paid for these two highly desirable developments: The level of unemployment and the size of the federal deficit will rise, possibly sharply.

The shape of the 1980s will depend on how calmly the administration and the Congress respond to these adverse short-run economic developments. Between 1965 and 1980 the U.S. missed three opportunities to stop the accelerating wave of inflation that began in 1965. In 1967, 1971, and again in 1977 the triumph of short-run political considerations over the needs of long-run policy led inexorably to an even higher rate of inflation on each successive upswing of the cycle.

The coming year, 1982, will present one more opportunity to eradicate inflation within the context of a free market, perhaps the last opportunity we will have to do so. If the government does not deviate from its major long-run goals, there is a high probability that starting in 1983 the U.S. economy will once again move into a sustainable period of fast and noninflationary expansion. But this outcome will require a triumph of long-run policy over short-run politics.

Will the president and his party be able to give ground gracefully in 1982 on two of their short-run objectives—fast economic growth *and* a reduced budget deficit—in order to ensure that the country achieves its ultimate goals: the eradication of inflation and the promotion of productivity growth within a system of free markets? The president's own assessment of the situation suggests that he is fully aware of the trade-offs involved and of the critical need to hold to a steady course: "If not now, when? If not us, who?"

READER'S GUIDE

MATTERS ECONOMIC have been at the forefront of recent discussions on national issues. One reason for this is that new thinking about economics and economic policy is lending an air of excitement to the subject. For the first time in a generation there is genuine controversy—and it covers virtually every aspect of the field.

In the first part of the Reader's Guide that follows I have tried to select a balanced list of ten books which discuss both facts and ideas relevant to the contemporary scene. All but one are recent publications, all were written for the intelligent layperson, and together they cover the spectrum of views on the political economy of the U.S. in the 1980s.

Facts, Views, and Analysis

The 1980s

1. Boskin, M.J. (editor). *The Economy in the 1980s: A Program for Growth and Stability.* Institute for Contemporary Studies, San Francisco, California. New Brunswick and London: Transaction Books, Rutgers, 1980.
2. Feldstein, M. (editor). *The American Economy in Transition.* National Bureau of Economic Research. Chicago and London: University of Chicago Press, 1980.
3. Rostow, W.W. *The World Economy, History & Prospect.* Austin and London: University of Texas Press, 1978.

The Liberal View

4. Galbraith, J.K. *The Age of Uncertainty.* Boston: Houghton Mifflin, 1977.
5. Keynes, J.M. *The General Theory of Employment, Interest and Money* (Chapter 24). New York: Harcourt Brace Jovanovich, 1965.
6. Pechman, J.A. (editor). *Setting National Priorities, Agenda for the 1980s.* Washington, D.C.: The Brookings Institution, 1980.

The Conservative or Supply-Side View

7. Friedman, M. & R. *Free to Choose: A Personal Statement.* New York and London: Harcourt Brace Jovanovich, 1979.

8. Kemp, J. *An American Renaissance: A Strategy for the 1980s.* New York: Harper & Row, 1979.
9. Wanniski, J. *The Way the World Works, How Economies Fail—and Succeed.* New York: Basic Books, 1978.

Energy

10. Stobaugh, R., and Yergin, D. (editors). *Energy Future.* Report of the Energy Project at the Harvard Business School. New York: Random House, 1979.

Sources of Current Information

The second part of this guide is a response to a question that I am frequently asked: What do you read to "keep up" with current developments?

Annual

1. *General economics.* The *Annual Economic Report of the President and the Council of Economic Advisers* (Government Printing Office), available each February, provides an excellent official summary of current and expectable developments in all major aspects of the U.S. economy. In addition, it provides a comprehensive statistical appendix that traces most economic and financial data series back to 1929. From time to time it provides insights into problems that are likely to emerge in the future, as well as clues to current thinking on how they should be resolved.

2. *Monetary matters.* For those more interested in the monetary, banking, and interest-rate aspects of economic events, *The Annual Report of the Board of Governors of the Federal Reserve System* provides a readable and definitive analysis of recent developments—both economic and monetary.

3. *International economics.* Developments in our economic relationships, which are covered in summary fashion in both of the reports cited above, are covered in greater detail in other annual reports:

• *The Annual Report of the International Monetary Fund* (Washington, D.C.).

• *The Annual Report of the Bank for International Settlement*, Basel, Switzerland, which is especially good on questions relating to the Eurodollar market.

Monthly

Several monthly magazines, official and unofficial, provide valuable insights—among them are:

1. *The Survey of Current Business:* The official monthly publication of

the U.S. Department of Commerce in which primary statistics on some of our most important economic series, such as national income, gross national product, and balance of payments, are presented and analyzed.

2. *The Federal Reserve Bulletin:* The official publication of the Federal Reserve System, in which primary statistics on our major monetary, banking, and interest-rate series are presented, developed, and analyzed.

3. Among the private monthly publications, most bank letters contain generally excellent analyses of the economic situation each month, along with special articles that are written with care for both accuracy and insight.

Weekly

The week has become a major cycle in our modern life and reading. A large number of economic publications are available on a seven-day cycle: *Business Week, U.S. News & World Report, Newsweek,* and *Time* are widely read by economists. A regular subscription to the *Economist* (a London weekly) provides a complete weekly overview of U.S. as well as international developments.

Daily

The *Wall Street Journal* is by far the outstanding economic daily paper available before breakfast in most U.S. cities.

If I had to pick just three private publications with which to "keep up," I would choose the *Wall Street Journal,* the *Economist,* and *Business Week.* People who live in the New York area might argue for the *Journal of Commerce* (daily) and the *New York Times.* Both provide an excellent coverage of economic events, but neither is available outside the New York area as rapidly as is the *Wall Street Journal.*

CREDITS

COVER   Drawing by Robert Graysmith. Reprinted by permission of Chronicle Features, San Francisco. Cover design by Mark Olson.

PAGE x   "Bomb threat." Drawing by Eric Smith. Courtesy Capital-Gazette (Md.) Newspapers.

PAGE 8   "He's considered to be a bellwether in the field of economic forecasting." Drawing by Stan Hunt; © 1978 The New Yorker Magazine, Inc.

PAGE 17   "Take it from me, Harlow, things are going to get a lot worse before they get better." Drawing by Whitney Darrow, Jr.; © 1974 The New Yorker Magazine, Inc.

PAGE 22   "Nervous, Kid?" Drawing by Chick Larsen. Courtesy *Richmond* (Va.) *Times-Dispatch*.

PAGE 29   "See your raise and raise you back." Drawing by Herblock. © 1979 Herblock from *Herblock On All Fronts* (New York: New American Library, 1980).

PAGE 38   ". . . And so, as the dollar sinks slowly in the west, we say farewell . . ." Drawing by Ray Osrin. © 1978 *Cleveland Plain Dealer*.

PAGE 43   Drawing by MacNelly. © 1979 *Chicago Tribune*. Reprinted by permission of the Chicago Tribune-New York News Syndicate, Inc.

PAGE 46   Drawing by M. Stevens; © 1981 The New Yorker Magazine, Inc.

PAGE 58   "Seriously, Paul . . . where are the brakes on this thing?" "Dead ahead." Drawing by MacNelly. © 1979 MacNelly in *The Richmond News Leader*. Reprinted by permission of the Chicago Tribune-New York News Syndicate, Inc.

PAGE 67   "It's a novel about interest rates." Drawing by Weber; © 1981 The New Yorker Magazine, Inc.

PAGE 74   "Fiddlin'." Drawing by Chick Larsen. Courtesy *Richmond* (Va.) *Times-Dispatch*.

PAGE 80   "Control Valve." Drawing by Don Hesse; © 1974 *St. Louis Globe-Democrat*. Reprinted by permission of L.A. Times Syndicate.

PAGE 84   Drawing by Tony Auth. Courtesy *Philadelphia Inquirer*.

PAGE 93   "Leader of the Free World." Drawing by Herblock. © 1979 Herblock from *Herblock On All Fronts* (New York: New American Library, 1980).

PAGE 106   "Gosh, how I envy you the future, son. Almost my whole life has been lived in a Keynesian context." Drawing by Donald Reilly; © 1981 The New Yorker Magazine, Inc.

PAGE 123   "Squeeze Play." Drawing by Art Wood. Courtesy *Farm Bureau News*.

PAGE 126   "You mean there's a limit to how many wishes I get?" Drawing by Herblock. © 1981 Herblock in *The Washington Post*.

PAGE 131   "I'm an Episcopalian on my mother's side and a supply-sider on my father's." Drawing by Dana Fradon; © 1981 The New Yorker Magazine, Inc.

PAGE 141   "There's no cause for panic, Mrs. Munson, but, frankly, there are certain indicators that cannot be ignored." Drawing by Chas. Addams; © 1979 The New Yorker Magazine, Inc.

PAGE 148   Photo of Ezra Solomon by Leo Holub.

Photo by Leo Holub

ABOUT THE AUTHOR

EZRA SOLOMON was born and raised in Burma, receiving an honors degree in economics from the University of Rangoon in 1940. Soon after his graduation, the Japanese Army occupied Burma and his family found itself trekking across the Chin hills into India, where he joined the Burma division of the British Royal Navy. After four years of active service, he was commander of a gunboat when a long-dormant fellowship for overseas graduate study materialized, bringing him to the University of Chicago in 1947 as a Burma State Scholar. While working toward his Ph.D. at Chicago, awarded in 1950, he joined the faculty of its Graduate School of Business, and was professor of finance from 1956 to 1960.

He has been at Stanford since 1961, when he was invited to be founding director of the International Center for the Advancement of Management Education. After the Center was established and running, Professor Solomon returned to full-time teaching and research as Dean Witter Professor of Finance at the Stanford Graduate School of Business—a position he still holds. In June 1971, he accepted a presidential appointment in Washington, D.C., as a member of the three-man Council of Economic Advisers, returning to Stanford in March of 1973.

Professor Solomon's expertise in the field of finance and economic policy has earned him visiting professorships in 12 foreign countries, and he has served as a consulting economist to government and industry here and abroad. He has written extensively, including ten books, one of which is a previous volume in The Portable Stanford series, *The Anxious Economy*. His best-known work, *The Theory of Financial Management*, is widely acknowledged as having had a major impact on the field both in the U.S. and abroad. He travels widely, and serves on the board of directors of six major U.S. companies, including Kaiser Aluminum, Foremost-McKesson, Sunbeam, United Financial, Capital Preservation Fund, and the Encyclopaedia Britannica, Inc.

He lives on the Stanford campus with his wife, Janet Cameron. They have three daughters, Shan, Ming, and Lorna.

INDEX